OUT OF THE FRYING PAN
INTO THE FIRE

This is the life story of
WAFL, VFL and SANFL Journeyman
Robert James (Bob) Beecroft

Bob Beecroft played League Football at the highest level for 16 years in three states. During his career, he was selected in an all-Australian side and is also a Hall of Fame inductee among many other football awards.

This is his life story from growing up in the bush and eventually realising his boyhood dream. This story told in his own words is at times harrowing, humorous and violent.

A story of one man's determination to achieve his dream and push on at all costs.

Now, in his seventies, he is retired and lives a peaceful life in Mount Baker, WA.

FOOTBALL ACHIEVEMENTS

1970   Best First Year Player League Football WAFL

1972   Best & Fairest Swan Districts Football Club
          Swan Medal

1972   All Australian Selection

1972, 1974, 1975, 1978, 1979 Represented WA (8 Games)

1977, 1978, 1979, 1980 Leading Goal Kicker Fitzroy FC VFL
          SDFC Team of the Century 1934-2000
          SDFC Life Membership 2000

Inducted into SDFC Hall of Fame in 2021

308 League Games
          126 SDFC Western Australia
          96 Fitzroy FC (VFL) Victoria
          86 Woodville (SANFL) South Australia
The game Tallies don't include official preseason and
night competitions, such as ESCORT Cup etc.
The inclusion of these games would take the Woodville
and Fitzroy tallies to over 100 games.

674 Goals

1978 Night Premiership defeating North Melbourne
      at Waverley
1979 VFL Record Winning margin vs Melbourne
      36.22 vs 6.12
      Kicked 10 Goals in VFL. Twice.

Country Football

Williams FC -1969 Fairest and Best

Moonta FC 1986 Fairest and Best

1986-1987 Leading Goal Kicker, Moonta Football Club

Encounter Bay FC

1988 Grand Finalist (Captain Coach)
1989 Premiers (Captain Coach)

Great Southern Football League

1988 Leading Goal Kicker—102 Goals
1989 Leading Goal Kicker—127 Goals
2021 Team of the Century Encounter Bay FC

Beecroft, Bob (author)
OUT OF THE FRYING PAN INTO THE FIRE
ISBN 9781922890382

Quinn Text Light 11/17
Cover and book design by Green Hill Publishing

1
THE EARLY YEARS

SHELLEY WALKED INTO THE BEDROOM, FLICKED ON THE LIGHT and told me to turn the radio off. This was the second time in the space of twenty minutes. I was listening to a talkback show, and I told her to turn the light off and go back to the patio, and to leave me alone. A few minutes later I turned the radio off and was dozing off to sleep. The bedroom door opened, and the light went on. Shelley was standing there with a 30cm butcher's knife. Then, holding it with both hands just above her head, she started walking towards me. By this time, I was wide awake and I told her to put the knife down. She said "No" and slowly kept coming towards me.

I had the top of the doona clutched in my left hand so that when she got close enough I could whip it off and defend myself. As she got within a metre, I ripped the doona off, spun to my right and kicked her in the sternum very hard. Shelley flew back into the built-in wardrobe and hit the floor. I jumped out of bed on the other side and picked up an umbrella, which had a long metal point on the end. Shelley was on her bum, but had managed to get hold of the knife again. I pleaded with her to put the knife down, but she refused. So I poked the umbrella into her left shoulder to protect myself. I thought momentarily of smashing her across the head with the umbrella but could not bring myself to do it. All the while, Shelley had a strange look on her face, and a cold stare. Right then, she lashed out with the knife as I had withdrawn the umbrella. The blade caught me on the right hand. I felt a stinging sensation and the blood was coming out quickly.

At that point, it was either go to town on her, or get out of the house. I chose the latter. I only had jocks on and went over the road to a Brethren family and asked them to call the police. They gave me a towel and called the police. This was to be the second-hardest period of my life, and it took at least 18 months to sort it out. The date of this incident was the 4th of June 2018. How the hell did it get to this, and why am I about to go through all the pain again?

I WAS BORN ON JANUARY 11TH, 1952, AT NARROGIN Hospital. Narrogin is a rural town located approximately 200 km southeast of Perth. It was established in the early 1900s and today it is home to over 4000 people. The town is surrounded by some of the best farmland in Western Australia, producing wool, grain, pigs, and so on. In its heyday, Narrogin was a major railway hub, but that has lessened with time. The town has all the amenities you would expect from a place this size, including hospitals, medical facilities, excellent sporting facilities, hotels, banks, supermarkets, and a myriad of shops. Narrogin had developed into a rural hub and today it is still a bustling, vibrant town with a rich history.

My father was James Alfred Morton (Jimmy) Beecroft, and he was a man of the land, a dinky-di Aussie who spent his entire working life on farms. His longest stint was with Aubrey Fowler, some 30 years or more. Together, Aubrey and his brother Tommy owned and ran quite a large farm and employed a lot of men to work the property. My earliest memories of this property date back to when I was five years old, some 65 years ago at the time of writing this book.

My mother was Maria Suseklis, a Latvian refugee who came to Australia in 1949 to escape the occupation of her country by the Germans and Russians. She was 26 years old. On her arrival in Australia, she was picked up from the wharf at Fremantle by Tommy Fowler and taken to Congelin Park to help with the Fowler household and their large family of seven children. It was during this time that Maria met Jimmy, and they eventually married.

Just prior to this, Dad spent a short time working on a property in Mount Barker, where I now live, and it was here at the age of four that I almost lost my life. My sister Ingrid was born 16 months before me on 10th of August 1950. I remember being in a shed with her, and she had a little teaset with small cups and plates. We were playing what we used to call Mothers and Fathers. I loved custard, so she decided to make some for me. The only problem was, she used yellow sheep dip powder and mixed it with water so that it looked like yummy custard. The main ingredients of this powder were arsenic, insecticides and fungicides. I ate some of this and we went back to the house. I started to vomit and was in a bad way. My mother grabbed Ingrid and was able to work out what had happened. I was in hospital very quickly. I still have memories of this green hose being shoved down my throat, time after time, and the never-ending vomiting and dry retching. It went on and on. My mother was told it was a close call and that I was very lucky to be alive. This is my very earliest childhood memory, and I never forgot the name Mount Barker. It's where it nearly all ended for me.

Congelin Park was an absolute circus, but it was exciting and there was always something happening. The property was 20-30 thousand acres and was situated approximately 20km northwest of Williams and 30km west of Narrogin.

Williams is a small town located on the Albany Highway, around 170km southeast of Perth and 30km from Narrogin. The population is roughly 1000 people, with around 350-400 living in the town. For a place of its size, Williams has excellent facilities. The rich farmland produces wool, grain, and cattle. Many travellers pass through the town and most stop to refuel, eat, or relax at one of three service stations, the hotel, or other eateries situated on the Albany Highway at Williams. The town also has a heritage trail which showcases some of its historic buildings.

The farm had its own general store and a large bunkhouse for the many men that worked there. A family also lived at the bunkhouse, and they did the cooking for the men. Our family lived in a house two or three kilometres from the store and bunkhouse. The farm had its own power supply generated by a huge diesel engine with a very large flywheel, which spun the alternator to create AC current. There was another house approximately 60 metres away from our house, and there was always a family living there. We stayed in this house until I was around 12 or 13, and then moved into another house two kilometres up the road, opposite an old hall.

Aubrey and Tommy did not get on. They fought each other constantly, and would have huge rows. A lot of the time, it was in front of the general store. Tommy kept pigs, which Aubrey despised, and a lot of arguments involved those pigs. The men would be given their jobs for the day by Aubrey and Tommy. This usually took place at the store and an argument would sometimes start between the brothers over who was going where. Those two could not agree on anything. Tommy was married to Gwen, who was a lovely and very well-organised woman, and they had a house about 600 metres from the bunkhouse.

Aubrey had what in those days would have been considered a mansion on top of a big hill. He was married to June, who considered herself a socialite and superior to everyone. She was a bitch whom I detested with a vengeance. They had three children: Penny, Flicky, and Jamie.

I remember a big party in front of the bunkhouse. It was for all the workers and their families. There were tables and chairs everywhere and the beer was flowing from 10-gallon kegs. I was around eight years old and there was a lot of noise. Near our table, a man bumped into another and accidentally spilled some beer over the other fellow. A fight erupted and suddenly there were tables, chairs, dust, and fists flying all over the place. Women were screaming and scattering with their children. It was absolute mayhem, and the noise and sound of smashing glass were horrific. When the brawl had subsided, I remember being in a room with about 30 men and my father was in the middle. Jimmy had some sort of managerial role at the property, and he was telling a bloke that he was sacked, and to be off the property come morning. Apparently, this fellow had pulled a knife, and that was a big no-no. In those times, the men all wore white shirts to celebrate anything, and I remember seeing a lot of blood all over the shirts, including my father's.

A lot of workers flowed through the property, including Italians, Poles, Slavs and many more. It wasn't unusual for the police to visit, as they were always looking for someone, and on numerous occasions, they found their man.

I remember June Fowler arriving at the store one morning, and she started to verbally get stuck into Alec Paul. Alec and his wife ran the store and Alec also worked on the farm a lot of the time. Alec didn't take kindly to the verbal assault and picked up a straw broom and began whacking June on the arse with it. This really set her off, so Alec started whacking her even harder, which resulted in June running out of the store and Alec right up her clacker getting as many hits as possible. He was yelling at her, "Get out of here, you fucking stupid bitch!" June made it to her car and got out of there in a hurry. I don't know what became of Alec after this incident, but I do know that June always got her way and would not have let this go.

I was about eight when Mum and Dad took Ingrid and me to visit Dad's sister, Aunty Lorna. She lived at Sabina Street, Mt Lawley, with her husband Fred Squires and their three boys, Fred, Robby, and Ray. On this trip we were accompanied by Harry Hanson, a very good family friend and an absolute gentleman, aged in his late sixties. Harry took me to the museum in Perth and we caught a bus to get there. We got off the bus at the museum and Harry said, "If I have to leave early, make sure you catch the same numbered bus and get off at Mount Lawley." He repeated the number a few times. I was so excited to get into the museum that the information went in one ear and out the other. I was enthralled by the museum and sure enough, Harry left early. I stayed for a fair while then went and caught the first bus that came along. I was trying to recognise where to get off, but nothing looked familiar. I ended up being the last one on the bus, and we were at the end of the run at Perry Lakes, of all places. The pig of a driver told me I would have to get off and that was it. No help whatsoever. When I look back, I always hope he had a prick of a life.

I started the long trek back to the city, guided by the skyscrapers. When I got into the city I just walked around and around, not knowing where I was. I stopped at a couple of shops and asked for a glass of water, which they kindly gave me. On my journey back to the city I had been offered a lift by a man, but I refused, as my mum had told us many times never to speak or go with strangers. By about 6 pm, I ended up sitting on the steps of the Norwood Hotel and bawling my eyes out. A kind gentleman tried to calm me down and took me into the kitchen, where the women there took over and eventually got me to speak. Apparently, the police had been alerted, because when the women contacted them, they knew all about me. I was taken back to Aunty Lorna's by the police. My mother was in a real mess by this stage, and everyone was in tears. I still get emotional to this day, sixty-odd years later, when I think back to that horrible day. The guy that offered me a lift reminds me of Eric Edgar Cooke, and that is a scary thought. I don't know why but I can still picture him and his car in my mind today.

Tommy and Aubrey's fights were getting worse and around the time I was nine or ten, they split the farm in two. I'm not sure who got what, but the two farms were a decent size and both families went on to prosper. My father went with Aubrey and stayed with him for the rest of his working life. My father had a very likeable personality and got on with everyone. This stood him in good stead with Aubrey. I found Aubrey Fowler to be a bombastic loudmouth who thought he could do what he liked just because he was Aubrey Fowler.

Not long before the split, I had gone out with the Hopper family. We were checking their numerous rabbit traps and it was just prior to dusk. The Hoppers had two girls; Vivian was about my age, and Gillian was three years older. They cooked for the men at the bunkhouse. When we got back to the bunkhouse, it was dark, and I was the first to enter. As I walked off the dirt onto the boards in front of the door, all hell broke loose. I was on the ground and my knees were hitting my chest like a piston. I could hear people yelling and screaming and heard a male voice say, "Get the fucking wire off him." Immediately, a man was on the ground doing exactly as I was. Both of us were in big trouble. Finally, someone was able to knock the wire away and stop the mayhem. Apparently, some of the workers had been playing soccer and knocked the wire down, and they just left it there live. At least that's what was told to my parents. I will never forget how strong that current was and how lucky I am to be here.

We always ate very healthy meals in those days. Mum and Dad had a big vegetable garden, and Maria was a superb cook. We didn't have a fridge, just a meat safe, and we had our own cow and churned our own butter. Washing was done in the outside laundry. A copper had a fire under it to heat the water, and alongside it were two large cement laundry troughs and a wringer to squeeze the water out of the clothes before they went onto the line for drying. Ironing was done with solid metal irons which had to be heated up on the stove. Everything about living in the 1950s was labour-intensive, and I loved it. The men and women worked hard and were very strong and fit. The children had to do their bit to help the family as well.

Respect, values, and honesty ruled, and there was no such thing as locking your vehicle. In fact, keys were left in the ignition and the house was always left unlocked. Ingrid and I had all sorts of pets including dogs, cats, lambs, rabbits, magpies, and a kangaroo. We also had a very aggressive ram that we had brought up from a lamb to full maturity. We had to be very careful around him because if he got you in his sights he would take off at a great pace and try and bunt you into next week. Ingrid and I would play games with the ram, and on a couple of occasions he caught up with us and we nursed sore arses for a week.

Tommy Fowler's son Dougal (Doogy) was about Ingrid's age. He had a veracious appetite and would eat everything in his lunchbox on the bus on the way to school. We had a huge fig tree in our yard and one day, Doogy came over to our place for a feed of figs. When he arrived, he headed straight for it. Just before he got into the figs, I told him to come and have a look at our pet ram. Rammy was about 150 metres away and we climbed over the fence and headed into the paddock. We were only about 50-60 metres in, and I could tell Rammy did not like what he saw. Poor Doogy had no idea, and by the time he grasped what was happening, Rammy was coming towards us at full pelt, and I had already taken off. Now, Doogy was not the quickest fellow on two feet and that day Rammy exposed that. I got to the fence with time to spare but unfortunately for Doogy, Rammy was gaining on him very quickly. When they arrived at the fence, Doogy was about two metres in front and as he desperately tried to get through the fence, Rammy gave him a hand. Doogy copped the biggest bunt up the arse I have ever seen, and went flying through the fence.

Ingrid and I could not stop laughing and Doogy was feeling very sorry for himself, holding his arse with both hands. He limped over to the fig tree, swearing at Rammy. Then he climbed to the top of the tree and started in on the figs. I have never seen anyone eat so many bloody figs in one sitting. After a while he stopped but a short time later, he was desperate to go to the toilet. However, nature had taken a turn for the worse. As he started frantically down the tree, he shat himself. Actually, he shat himself all the way down. He headed off home with a sore arse and shit everywhere. The poor bugger had about a kilometre to walk before he got home. I'm not sure how he handled it when he got home, but Ingrid and I never saw Doogy at our place ever again.

Aubrey Fowler's son, Jaime, was a couple of years older than me and one day I ended up at their house helping to mark out the asphalt tennis court with Aubrey and Jaime. I was around 10 years old at the time. If I didn't have the board or string at the right spot, they would start to humiliate me with Aubrey saying things like, "I don't think the kid's got a lot of brains." Or: "By gee, he's timid this kid, isn't he?" They carried on like this as though I wasn't even there. I remember walking down the hill on the way home with tears rolling down my face and a huge hatred for Aubrey and Jaime Fowler. The only ones I would have any time for in that family were Penny and Flicky, whom I considered great girls.

In 1963 or 1964 we moved into another house on the farm. It was a kilometre or so up the road, opposite an old hall, and was at the entry to the farm. The 14-stand two-storey shearing shed was two or three hundred metres away. The big farm sheds were 150 metres behind it, and a large bunkhouse was on a hill 70 metres from the shearing shed.

It wasn't long after this that Aubrey bought himself a plane. It was a Cessna and he set about getting himself a licence, which he eventually achieved. He used to fly to Perth quite often, and on one occasion he was refused permission to land at the time he was ready to do so. He was extremely arrogant and had a loud annoying voice, and said to control: "I'm Aubrey Fowler and I am landing my plane now." And he did. I don't know what the ramifications were; I was never told.

Aubrey liked to change his cars pretty often, and on one occasion he went to Perth and picked up a brand-new Studebaker, which was an American vehicle. Studebakers were built in Melbourne from 1960-1966. He arrived back at the farm and the vehicle had gouges, scratches, and dents all the way along the sides. Apparently, he arrived at the Dwarda Bridge at the same time as a truck. The bridge is fairly narrow, so you had to cross it one vehicle at a time. Well, Aubrey had other ideas and would not give way to the truck. The truck kept going, and Aubrey's new car was no longer new.

My mother used to clean, wash, and iron for June Fowler, to bring in some extra money. My mother would break down in tears when she tried to explain to Ingrid and me about what took place in Latvia. I know it affected her badly, but unfortunately Ingrid and I were too young to be of much help with this situation. Sometimes she would get so depressed that she would go on a bender and drink for four or five days just to kill the pain. It was on one of these occasions that she actually walked to Narrogin, some 30km away, and stayed with friends in town for a whole week. I was only young and really felt the effects of my mother not being home, and I remember being really upset and angry when she got back. Thankfully this didn't occur too often, and she was the best mother Ingrid and I could have ever had.

Mum and Dad rarely drank alcohol at home but they would get into a few when we went into town shopping, which was every three to four weeks. The shopping trips were very interesting. Once a month we would head into Narrogin at about 10am. Mum would have us all dressed up, the whole family neat as a pin. We would do a mountain of shopping, enough to last for the month. In those days money went a long way. A long neck (large bottle of beer) was around 40c, a stamp 5c, petrol was about 8c per litre, and the cost of a new house was about $20,000. My father cleared around $186 per month in 1965-66. I only know this because I saw one of his pay cheques. After all the shopping was done, the line of full boxes of groceries was stacked up along the wall at the entry to the Duke of York Hotel. Let me tell you, it was some line.

Ingrid and I had the joy of guarding the groceries. Dad would give us some money and then he and Mum would head off into the pub. As on all these trips, his last words before going in were, "Okay, kids, look after the groceries. Your mother and I won't be long." Ingrid and I knew it would be a good four or five hours before we would see them again. We would take turns to go and buy some fish and chips, and settle in to mind the groceries. Every now and again, some bloke would walk by and make some comment about the magnitude of shopping stacked along the wall. Usually around 4-5pm, the Salvation Army people would arrive and set up on the other side of the steps leading into the hotel. One would have a trombone, another a set of drums, and someone else a tambourine. They would play and sing their hymns for at least an hour. Towards the end, one would go into the pub and collect as much money as possible from the drinkers. I liked the Salvos and still do, but I can honestly say I didn't like their singing from such close quarters.

Mum and Dad would eventually come out and we then stacked all the groceries into the car. I've no idea how we got them all in, but we did. We would then head over to the Cornwall Hotel for a final session, which usually lasted a couple of hours. We would park outside Steve's Deli, which was directly over the road from the hotel. Ingrid and I would go into Steve's and buy something to eat and then go in again and grab an ice cream or some lollies. We only got these once a month, so we made the most of it.

Mum and Dad would eventually come out of the pub, and it was off home. Now, this was another adventure entirely. By this stage, both of my parents had consumed a fair amount of wallop and were somewhat inebriated. Usually about 10km out of town, the old man's driving would have gone from erratic to no damn good at all. One section of road had sloping banks and we would be up on the bank, and Ingrid and I would be going right off in the back seat. So Dad would stop, and Ingrid would drive us home. She did this from around the age of ten or eleven, as Dad had taught her to drive at an early age. When the old man was in this state, he drove very slowly, thank God.

I guess because we only went to town once a month, Mum and Dad took the opportunity to sink a few just as Ingrid and I took the opportunity to get into some lollies and ice cream. My mother and father worked very hard, so looking back I couldn't blame them at all.

Mum would always buy a bottle of sherry to take home and ask the old man if he wanted to buy one. His answer was always the same, "Christ no, I don't want any of that rot gut." We would get home and unload the groceries. They wouldn't get put away until next day, although by this time we had a kerosene fridge, so the fridge stuff was put away that night. As always, Dad would grab the bottle of sherry and take a few swigs, which would send my mother off immediately. Mum had an accent and a Latvian temper and would verbally unload on Dad. She would make a growling noise and say, "Give me da pucken bottle! Get your own, you silly pool." And then she would guard it with her life. To this day I don't know why the old man just didn't buy his own—it would have saved him some grief.

Drinking and driving was a normal occurrence in those days, and I remember going to Williams Primary School on the bus one morning and seeing a white ute lying in the paddock on its roof. I recognised the ute immediately as Tommy Fowler's. Tommy had been at the Williams Country Club, and had driven home after a big session. The paddock was on Fred Bell's property and Tommy had staggered to their place for assistance, and apparently did not have a scratch on him. Tommy was a really good bloke, but when he got on the wallop there were no half measures with him. Whether he had a piss or a spew after consuming too much, he would always say, "What a bloody waste of good beer."

Before we had moved into the second house, I had found a 44-gallon drum which had been cut in half longways. I thought it would make a good canoe and somehow got it to the Blue Dam. This was a big dam, and it had a windmill which pumped water into a tank. The drum was unstable in the water so you had to balance and keep very still, otherwise it would tip over. Ingrid was with me, so I gave it a go in the shallows and it was okay. For some reason, Ingrid pushed me out into the deep and then went home, which was about a kilometre away. All would have been okay, but I could not swim at this stage of my life; so I just sat there, deadly still, and shat myself. About half an hour later, Mum appeared over the bank and swam out to get me. She guided the drum to shore, and I got out. She was not happy and said, "Pucken silly kits." I knew this wasn't the end of it.

At about 6pm, Ingrid and I jumped into the bath. When we were young, we bathed together to save water. My mother appeared with a sapling off a tree which was about the size of a school cane. She hauled Ingrid up by one arm and laid into her, delivering six or seven lashes, which would have been quite painful. Ingrid was crying and Mum just walked out and got on with what she was doing. I looked at Ingrid and said, "You silly bitch, you deserved that." She couldn't answer because she was too busy crying. Dad left Mum the job of delivering any corporal punishment required where Ingrid and I were concerned, and I can honestly say that every time we copped it, we deserved everything we got.

Ingrid and I ran amok all over the property and I remember getting her to help me lay some rabbit traps about 1.5km from the house. I had around a dozen traps plus a big dingo trap which I had found. We laid the rabbit traps and I decided to lay the dingo trap as well. I was having trouble as the thing was so big. All of a sudden it snapped onto my leg, and we couldn't budge the trap. Ingrid was screaming and I told her to run home and get the old man. She took off and I remember the pain was killing me. It wasn't long before Dad was there in the ute. He got out and extracted my leg from the dingo trap. The relief was instant, but it was a while before the leg felt normal again.

The old man said, "What the hell are you doing with a dingo trap? There's no bloody dingos around here." I was in no mood to talk and just said, "Dunno."

15

Life in the second house was pretty good and I started spending a lot of time over at Tommy Fowler's place. They all loved my mother and really appreciated her for what she had done for their family. I hung around a lot with Tommy's son Benny, who was about two years younger than me. I was about twelve at this stage.

Mum saved up for ages so that she could buy me a bike. Our family didn't have a lot in the way of money, but we had a good healthy life. I used to go to primary school in Williams and would wear shorts and a short-sleeved shirt, and bare feet as I hated shoes. In winter the puddles of water would be solid ice, but I never felt cold at that age. Mum had given up buying school jumpers for me as I would continually lose them and they were expensive to replace, but it never bothered me as I ran full pelt wherever I went.

On the weekends, all my time was spent with Benny Fowler, and in the winter the paddocks between our houses were white with ice, or frost as we called it. The houses were a couple of kilometres apart, so I would take off as fast as I could go to get over to Benny's as quickly as possible. I could feel my feet starting to numb with the cold and by the time I made it to Benny's, they were blue. I would sit near the heater until my feet returned to normal.

The bike Mum bought me relieved a lot of this pain, but caused me other pain. You see, she had bought me a racing bike with skinny slick tires. It was built for speed, and terribly equipped to deal with the gravelly country roads. I came a cropper (fell off) so many times that I thought I would never get the hang of it. Eventually it all came together, and I got to master the bike quite well. One setback was when I wanted to show Ingrid how well the brakes worked. I rode flat out towards the brick wall of the house but applied the brakes a little late. The bike smashed into the wall with a thud, and I followed it. I picked myself up, feeling sore and sorry. I looked over to the bike to find the front wheel was now pushed right in towards the axle and resembled a half circle. The bike was out of action for a couple of months but eventually we got it fixed.

It was around this time that Jimmy's brother (my Uncle Bob) moved into the house next to ours (the first house) with his wife Gwen and my cousins Patricia, Yvonne, and Chris. Gwen was a smallish lady with a quick temper, and I always considered her to be a bit nuts. One day she had a crack at me, and I laughed. Next thing, she came out with a large butcher's knife and started chasing me with the knife in her hand. I would run, then stop to let her catch up, and take off again. Ingrid ran to get Mum, and she got to Gwen who was huffing and puffing at this stage. My mother was furious with Gwen and said, "What the puck are you doing to my son, you puckin silly bitch?" I told my mum not to worry. The stupid bitch couldn't catch me anyways. Mum told me to be quiet and to get inside the house. Apparently, she gave Gwen a real rollicking and took the knife from her and everything just went back to normal.

Not too long after we had moved into our second house, Uncle Bob and Aunty Gwen split up and Uncle Bob moved to Broomehill, a town on the Great Southern Highway between Katanning and Albany. He joined Main Roads and stayed there for the rest of his working life. My cousins Patricia, Yvonne, and Chris lived with us for about nearly 12 months while Uncle Bob got back onto his feet and settled. This was a hard time for our family, with three more kids to bring up, as my parents had to pay for everything. Now and again Uncle Bob would give Dad some money, but it was nowhere near enough. Somehow we battled through, and my cousins were always grateful for what my parents did for them.

One time I had slicked my hair back with Brylcreem, a ghastly oily white cream which would become clear once applied. A 100km-per-hour wind would not move your hair once this stuff was applied. I was trying to copy Elvis, and Yvonne wanted me to make some scones as Mum was out somewhere. I thought why not and got the dough going, and then layered the sink with lots of flour. The dough was rolled into balls and then I slammed them down into the flour, mimicking my mother as I was doing so: "You want puckin scones I give you puckin scones." There was flour from arse-hole to breakfast time, and I would turn and give Yvonne a grin as this was happening. The flour had gone all over my hair and face and by this time Yvonne was doubled up on the floor and out of control with laughter. Ingrid, Patricia, and Chris joined in and then we were all out of control. The scones got thrown out because they were a disaster, but we cleaned the kitchen up and Mum didn't know anything about the scone making.

Money was tight and Aubrey was usually late paying Dad his monthly cheque. I have no idea why, as they lived an opulent lifestyle and had everything. I always felt that June and Aubrey treated my family as slaves and I really resented this. Mum would always ask Dad if Aubrey had paid him yet and Dad would say, "No, but don't worry, he will pay me soon." This would sometimes go on for a couple of weeks and then Mum would explode. She would pick up the phone and ring Aubrey.

"Where's my kusband's money you pucken bastard? Why you not gib he his pucken money?"

She would slam the phone down and storm out of the house and up the hill to the mansion. About half an hour later Mum would be back with his cheque. She would wave it in the air and say, "Here your money you wik bastard." The old man would just give a grin and put the cheque into his pocket.

There would be times that Aubrey would leave his house rather than face Maria when she was in this frame of mind. My mother and father loved each other to death but even the old man didn't want to be around when Mum lost it. That Latvian temper was a beauty.

It was around five o'clock one day and Mum still hadn't come home. She had been up at June and Aubrey's place cleaning and ironing since around ten that morning. June and Aubrey had gone away for a few days so Ingrid and I decided to head up the hill to see where Mum had got to. We got to the mansion and went inside. We were greeted with, "Kullo kits." (Hello kids). It took me about two seconds to work out what was going on here. There was a substantial bar in the living room at the base of the staircase with every alcoholic drink you could imagine, and the old woman had had a swig of just about everything on offer. She was showing the effects and had the wobblies up by the time Ingrid and I arrived on the scene.

We both yelled at her, "What the hell are you doing, Mum?"

By this stage, Maria did not give a damn and just said, "Puk dem, dey hab plenty." And then she started singing Latvian songs, which used to drive me mad. Ingrid and I then had to get her out of the house and somehow down the hill and home. This happened more than once. The episodes didn't happen very often, but we knew if Mum was up at June and Aubrey's while they were away, then there was cause for concern. Looking back, I find it quite funny because Mum and Dad were underpaid for the work they did. The irony of it all, though, was that if Ingrid or I ever did anything wrong or dishonest we would cop it, and rightly so.

I loved spending time over at Benny Fowler's place, and Benny and I became good mates. Tommy and Gwen had a nice old home with a big verandah, a tennis court, and a beautiful little orchard near the front. At the back entry to the home there was a hessian waterbag which hung from the rafters. It was cylindrical in shape and held approximately 20 litres of drinking water. The canvas-hessian bags kept water cool by way of evaporation as the breeze was blowing on them, and there was a hose and a drinking cup attached. I always remember how cold and beautiful the water was, and that everyone used the same cup, no big deal at all. All the homes had some form of water bag hanging on the verandah and it was rare to see a vehicle driving around the farm without one hanging off it, at the front or side.

Gwen, Benny's mum, was all natural class and ran a tight ship when it came to the home. Benny would always have chores which had to be done before we could go off and do our own stuff. I used to give him a hand with the jobs and then we would be off. Sometimes I would dink Benny (give him a lift) on my bike but after a few crashes I decided to leave the bike at his place, and we walked or ran everywhere. Benny had a cattle pit (railway line laid parallel a few inches apart, and about three metres wide) at the bottom of the driveway and a lot of gravel stones to boot. This was usually the place we came to grief. We would be going too fast, hit the cattle pit then the gravel, all while trying to turn, and off we would come. After a few of these crashes, Benny would not let me dink him anywhere.

I have very fond memories of times spent with Benny and the Tommy Fowler family. For Benny and me, it was like a boys' own adventure manual, and we did everything you would imagine two boys of our age would do out in the country, in the fresh air. We built a nice tree house down at the creek and spent time there. I went there by myself a lot of times and watched the birds right next to me. I remember the tree house being such a peaceful place, with just the sound of the birds, and running water below.

In the winter, when the creek would swell, we would make a canoe out of corrugated iron. We used tar to seal it up and built a side stabiliser so the canoe would not flip over. Except for a few leaks, it worked well. We built an underground cubby in the middle of a paddock with a trapdoor. It was about two metres square and deep enough to sit in. A couple of ledges and two candles to see, and you were in another world.

Then Benny and I found an old tank, not far from the hall. It had been lying there discarded for quite a while. The tank was fairly big, a typical round rainwater tank found on most houses of that era. We rolled the tank against the trunk of a huge white gum tree, which was only a few metres away from the edge of the road. I found some old wire rope and secured a piece of wood to one end. The timber (a tree branch) was half a metre long. I climbed up the tree and secured the other end to a huge limb that extended out over the road. Once you got onto the top of the tank, you grabbed the handle and swung way out over the road and landed back on the tank. It was like a trapeze in the circus. The swing was exhilarating, and I spent hours on the thing. I would use it in the mornings while waiting for the school bus. But Ingrid and Benny would never use the swing, no matter how hard I tried to cajole them into doing so.

I quite often had a meal over at Benny's place, usually lunch. Gwen would have lunch organised and it would mostly be a nice hot meal followed by sweets. The entire family of nine plus me would be seated around a magnificent dining table which was situated in the dining room directly opposite the kitchen. The table was set out beautifully and just before we ate our meal a member of the family would say grace. Gwen was a stickler for etiquette; that is, respect, honesty and consideration of others, which I find sadly lacking in today's society. There was a correct way to eat and the way the knife and fork was left on the plate at the end of a meal was also done a certain way.

The conversation involved all members of the family, was intelligent, and at times humorous. I was very shy in my early years so I rarely spoke at occasions like this. I learnt a lot about etiquette from the Tommy Fowler family and they also had a correct way of speaking. The "g" was not left off words and the English language was spoken correctly. I found all of this rather fascinating. The other thing about this family which impressed me was the fact everything was organised and the whole show ran like clockwork. This was due to Gwen and looking back, I guess with seven children one would have to be organised.

At home, Mum was always onto Ingrid and myself about manners and the way we conducted ourselves, but alas sometimes this would go out the door with Ingrid and myself. Even so, we would never interrupt adults when they were talking and if we had to it would be "excuse me" first. In those days, kids were to be seen and not heard.

Either Mum or Dad would milk our cow, but Ingrid and I were not allowed near it. The cow had a tendency to be aggressive and on a few occasions I would see the milk bucket flying through the air after a vicious back kick. There would be milk all over the place and the old man would be mad as hell, delivering swear words that I didn't even know existed. Sometimes he would end up with milk all over his face. When the cow started to move, it was time to get nervous and get ready.

June Fowler would drive down the hill every couple of days and knock on our door. She would produce a milk billy which my mother would fill with fresh milk, and off back up the hill she would go. One morning there was a knock on the door and there was June with her billy. I was about thirteen at this time, and told her there was no milk today as Mum was helping Dad with sheep and the cow had not been milked, but it would be that night. June got extremely annoyed and told me to go and milk the cow. I explained that my parents would not allow this, and she got even more annoyed. She told me I should be ashamed of myself and that I had better start milking the cow.

As it was, I hated the sight of June Fowler and I decided there and then not to take her shit anymore. I told her we were not her slaves and if she wanted milk, to go and get her own bloody cow and get her spoiled brat of a son to milk it. I then turned around and went inside, slamming the door. Sure enough, that night the phone rang and it was June. Dad answered and he yelled out, "Maria, June is on the phone." Mum got stuck into June and I never heard another word about the incident. June was a very good-looking woman, a stunner really, but she had such a superior attitude and treated workers like garbage. If only she'd had Gwen's personality, then she would have been the complete package. June and I were like a red rag to a bull with each other and it was never going to be any different.

By this time, I had started high school at Narrogin and Benny had headed off to school in Perth. All the Fowlers, including Aubrey's children, attended either Hale School, or in the girls' case it was St Hilda's in Perth. Both schools were exclusive private schools and rather expensive. I saw a lot less of Benny after he started at Hale and I really missed him as we had always hung around together and done so much. We used to do a lot of horse riding and then swim the horses in the dams and race bareback to the house. Everything we did was fun and now it all came to an end. This left me feeling alone and empty for a fair while, but like anything in life, you must deal with it and move on.

I started to help Dad a lot more but still did the boyhood things. Dad and I were out top dressing with an old Thames truck one day, and I was on the back filling the hopper with superphosphate while he drove the truck. The ride was extremely bumpy, and you had to be very careful on the back otherwise you would end up on your arse in the middle of the paddock. It was good for teaching balance. On one of these occasions the old man and I ran out of water, so we walked into the bush, and he picked out a particular spot. "Right," he said. "We need to dig a hole here, down about a foot and a half." Well, we dug the hole and waited about ten minutes and sure enough up came the water. "Now wait ten minutes more and there will be enough to drink." We had a good drink and got back into the top dressing and then headed back to the sheds near home. Job done.

Another job was getting firewood. We would collect the wood then take it back to the sheds at the main part of the farm, and saw the wood into small logs approximately 350cm long. This was done by using a tractor hooked up to a big circular saw. The saw spun by way of a long belt which was put over a pulley of the tractor and a pulley on the saw. In this case,

24

the tractor was an old Alice Chalmers, which had to be cranked up by hand. Cranking up a tractor by hand was very dangerous and had to be done in a certain way, otherwise you could get yourself into big trouble. I never attempted this until I was about fifteen. Once we had cut the logs and stacked them onto the truck, we would drive to the shearing shed and unload the wood. I would be up on the truck and the old man would be on the ground stacking the wood.

On this particular day, I was in a hurry and got stuck into getting this load off as quickly as possible. Wood was flying all over the place. On several occasions, Dad would yell out "Hey, watch where you throw that bloody wood!" Some of the logs had only missed him by 200mm, and he was starting to get annoyed with me. I soldiered on, and suddenly I heard a clonk. Looking down, I saw the old man grab the front of his head, swearing profusely. I knew it was time to vacate the scene at the rate of knots, so off I went. I was off the truck and over the first fence with the old man in hot pursuit. I had two more fences to clear, then 250 metres to the house. I had a huge leap and could run and jump over fences head-on, barbed wire and all. I was over the fences in no time, but the old man had to climb through them. This gave me a big advantage and the old man had given up the chase at the second fence. I tore into the house and Mum was in the kitchen.

"What da kell is wrong mit you son?"

I said, "The old man wants to kill me." And I explained to her what had happened.

"Don't worry about a ting, son. I will pix him."

It was a nervous wait, but a few hours later the old man got home and walked into the kitchen. I got the shock of my life when I looked at his bald head. Halfway between the middle of his head and his forehead there was a huge lump. You could fit an egg cup over it and the base of the lump had already turned a bluey-black colour.

Mum said, "What you done to your ked, Jimmy?" And with that she burst into fits of laughter. I joined in because it was such a sight. Then the old man started to laugh, and it ended up a jolly old time.

Tommy Fowler would call into the house every now and then and ask Maria if he could borrow me to help him round up sheep and bring them in from the back paddocks into the shearing shed. Sometimes this could be a few kilometres. I would take my football and kick it around the sheep to keep the mob together. It was all running and kicking, and I loved it. Tommy really appreciated it and would drop me home and thank me for my efforts.

Now and again, I would give Dad a hand to fill the big diesel motor which supplied the farm's power generator with diesel fuel. On one of these occasions, we walked into the shed housing the motor and were both stunned to see a fellow asleep on the concrete floor. The noise from the motor was very loud and I found it hard to fathom how anyone could possibly sleep there. Dad woke him up and I was immediately taken aback by how handsome the young man was. He was the spitting image of Elvis Presley, about six feet tall, and was dressed in a thick full-length khaki coat and black boots. Dad took him outside and they chatted for around fifteen minutes. Then we took him up to the bunkhouse, where he was given a hot meal and a room. Dad arranged for him to work on the farm.

Ingrid and I travelled to and from Narrogin High School by bus, and the trip would take over an hour by the time the bus picked up all the other kids. I hated school. For me it was all about the sport, and even though I did okay with the school-work I had to labour through it all. One of the reasons for this may have been my poor eyesight. An optometrist visited the school one time and tested the eyesight of all the students.

After testing my eyes, he looked at me and said, "Do you play sports, son?"

I replied, "Yes."

"Do you play any ball sports?" I told him I played cricket and football.

There was a brief pause and he looked at me again and said, "How can you see the ball?"

I told him I could see the ball no worries. He shook his head and said he didn't know how I could with such poor eyesight. It turns out that I had bad stigmatisms on both eyes. I couldn't read what was on the blackboard very well, but thought I could see the footy and cricket balls okay. I ended up wearing glasses, but my poor eyesight became a problem right throughout my football career. It was a problem I just had to deal with as best as I could.

In the first year of high school (I was thirteen years old) I was approached by Gary Fairhead, who was a couple of years older than me and was from Williams. Gary had been watching me kick the footy around at school and asked me to play C Grade (under 16) for Williams. This was about two months before the 1965 season began. I hadn't played competitive football up to this point and was as keen as mustard to get into it. So I said yes.

I had a couple of problems to overcome before it became a reality. The first one was how to get to training, and the second was that I didn't have any football boots. I discussed it with Mum and Dad, and we came up with a solution. Once a week I could catch the Williams school bus, and Dad would pick me up after training. It was approximately 20 kilometres from the farm to Williams.

Dad got me a job on the farm during the school holidays, so for two weeks I picked up and stacked mallee roots (gnarled pieces of wood ripped up during the process of ploughing paddocks ready for sowing of crops) and rocks. Once I had many piles of mallee roots stacked into heaps, I would take a bucket of coals and set them all alight. The big, ploughed paddocks would have smoke billowing from the mallee roots and you could see the flames at night, as the roots burned for a long time. The work was hard as I would start at seven thirty in the morning and finish at five or six o'clock. I would take my lunch and a bottle of water. Jaimie Fowler would be in the comfort of a tractor and have his lunch delivered.

I used to look across the paddock and tell myself that I was the one getting stronger every day, and it made me super determined to keep going, plus I desperately needed to buy my footy boots. At the end of the two weeks, Dad handed me three guineas (three pounds three shillings) which Aubrey had given him for my two weeks of work. In 1965, this was more than enough money to buy a good pair of football boots. I bought my boots from Parry's store which was situated in the main street of Narrogin, and they are still there today. The boots were Gold Star brand and were a high-cut boot covering the ankle. They had aluminum stops, white laces, and a hard toe. I was over the moon and couldn't wait to try them out. I loved the boots, but they would be termed cumbersome in today's football world. No matter, they did the job for me.

One of my good mates at high school was Charlie Burnett. Charlie was very confident and had a mature body for his age. He was also a very good footballer and was quick for his height. We both played C Grade for Williams, and Charlie was playing A Grade at 15 years of age. Charlie had tried out for the State Schoolboys at 14 and had come very close to making the WA side.

He pulled me aside one day at school and said, "Mate, you need to try out for the State schoolboys. I reckon you would make it, so let's go to the staffroom and talk to Mr Humphries."

Humphries was the Phys Ed teacher at school, and you had to get his permission. He came to the door and Charlie put my case to him. After Charlie had finished, Humphries looked at me and said, "No, Charlie, he's too skinny and it would be a waste of time. So, the answer is no."

Charlie had another go but to no avail. We both walked off with Charlie saying, "What a fucking prick."

I said, "Don't worry about it, mate; thanks for sticking up and trying for me." I then stopped, looked at Charlie and said, "I'm going to make that bastard eat his words one day." I have no doubt that Humphries would have thought about this encounter in the following years when I achieved what I did in football.

One incident I remember at school also involved Charlie. We had a maths teacher named Eric Alcock. Eric was a no-nonsense whirlwind on two feet. He was about 40 years old and would storm into the classroom, throw his Gladstone bag against the wall and start writing on the blackboard. All done in around five seconds. Eric also liked to dish out a lot of homework, as did a few of the other teachers. There were about 30 of us, and we were all whining about the amount of homework, so before Eric came In, Charlie suggested to the class that he would have a word to him about the amount of homework being given.

We all agreed, and Charlie said, "I want all of you bastards to back me up on this."

We all said, "No worries, mate."

And then Eric stormed in and the Gladstone bag hit the wall with a thud. He was writing furiously on the board when there was an Excuse me sir from the room. Eric turned around abruptly and glared at Charlie, who was now standing up to address the issue.

"Yes, Burnett," said Alcock.

Charlie put our case forward and Eric now had steam coming out of his ears. Eric raised his loud voice and asked, "Who else amongst you lot agree with Burnett?"

I put my hand up and Eric glared at me. I looked around and there wasn't a single other hand in the air.

Eric quickly fixed a mad gaze onto Charlie and yelled, "Sit down, Burnett, and stop wasting my time."

Eric wasn't going to waste one second of his life. It was as if he was watching his biological clock ticking away the seconds. He had no patience at all. During this lesson, Eric asked the class for an answer to a maths question and a few hands shot into the air. Eric pointed at a student named Dennis Hastie. Dennis was a good fellow but the poor bugger had a bad stutter. Dennis started to try and spit the answer out and started to stutter badly.

'The c.c.c.com..com..n.n.n.d.d.d...'

I felt so bad for him and then Eric screamed, "Sit down Hastie," and pointed to another student for the answer.

Talk about cruel, but that was Eric not-a-second-to-waste Alcock. When the class was over and Eric had left, Charlie stood up and called the class a weak mob of pricks. I still have a laugh about that incident now. You never know who has your back until the shit hits the fan. It's still the same today.

My first year of competitive football went really well and I could hardly wait for the next season to start. I was fourteen and in second year high school. Whenever we played away, the Fairhead family used to give me a lift from Williams to places like Boddington, Darkan, and so on. Gary and Kim Fairhead's father, Lou, was right into football and was a big help to me. Lou took me down to Perth with his boys on a couple of occasions to watch East Perth play, as he was a devoted East Perth man. I found watching that couple of games to be exhilarating and it lit a fire in my belly. I wanted desperately to one day be out there.

It was around this time that Dad took me to the one and only game of league football that I attended with him, which happened to be a final between Perth and East Perth. Dad had a friend in Perth who drove us to Subiaco from Mount Lawley, but not before they got stuck in at a pub near the ground. I waited patiently outside the pub, and I could hear the crowd roaring as the game got underway. I was getting really anxious and annoyed. Eventually the old man and his mate came out, and off we went. His mate, being half full of wallop, drove the wrong way up a one-way street, but we got to the ground and went inside. The place was packed and we were able to squeeze in on the hill, all grass and no seats. It didn't matter. The atmosphere was electric and I watched in awe as the likes of Barry Cable, Mal Atwell, Kevin Murray and a young Malcolm Brown were doing their stuff. I had pins and needles all over my body and remember saying to the old man, "I'm going to play here one day." He just smiled and said, "That's good." That day really stirred up the footy emotions in me and I can still see those pictures in my mind's eye when I think back to it all.

At 15, when I was in my third year of high school, I was picked for the Narrogin High School side to play against a visiting school side. I was really thrilled as most of the players were one to two years older than me, but that didn't even matter as all I wanted to do was play and play well. The excitement was unreal. Game day came around and the game was on. I took a couple of early big grabs paying in the backline and really felt at home. Then tragedy struck. I sat on top of a pack and took a screamer and still had the ball when I hit the ground. On the way down, an opponent had taken my feet from under me. All of my weight was on my left elbow when I hit the ground—and I mean ground, as there were very few turf ovals in those days. I felt the elbow go; the sensation was as if it was sliding along my forearm and then was in the palm of my hand. That's how it felt, and then came the searing pain. I screamed in agony and was taken straight to hospital. After I came out of the theatre, I remember seeing my mother standing at the side of the hospital bed and crying, and I looked at my left arm and saw it was extremely swollen.

Next day, Mum was there when the doctor came into the room to talk to us both. The first thing he said was, "Well, you won't ever play football again, son." I was in shock and didn't hear anything else he said.

After I was discharged from hospital I remember very vividly saying to Mum, "I will play football again, Mum, I promise you."

Mum told me not to worry about anything and do what the doctor says. The injury took me a long time to get over; even to get full movement back took months. I found an old axle with two rims on it in the bush. It was about a metre and a half wide and it wasn't too heavy, just right in fact. I don't know what the axle was from, but it was a gift from God for me. I used it every day, doing numerous lifting exercises, most of which I got out of a book from school, and my arm started to improve dramatically. As well as getting normal movement back, I was building up good strength.

Third Year was a complete write-off for me as far as sport was concerned, but now I set myself to be playing footy again at 16. Even all these years later, 55 years at the time of writing this book, you can still see the smashing my elbow took. But to be honest, the arm is very strong and has taken everything that has been thrown at it over all this time. It's quite amazing, really.

Life on the farm went on. I would sometimes go up to the main sheds and help Cedric Andrews. Cedric was in charge of the machinery side of the farm. He was a brilliant welder, and he could and would make anything out of steel for the farm. He made grain bins for the trucks, big trailers—you name it, he made it. Cedric had a good personality. He was a solidly built man, around 5'10" tall, and he wore glasses. I would hold steel in place while he welded, sweep the shed floor, and other odd jobs that he got me to do. I never got paid for this work but I didn't mind doing it for nothing as I liked Cedric and was only too pleased to help him out.

On one occasion, the farm semi-trailer pulled into the sheds, having just returned from Perth after delivering a load of grain, which would usually be oats or wheat. The truck was driven by an Italian named Libby. He had a very happy personality and was always laughing or smiling, sometimes whistling or singing too, and he reminded me of Liberace, the flamboyant American entertainer. Libby jumped out of the semi and was holding a little black and white kitten which apparently had found its way into the truck while in Perth. That was the story, anyhow.

"Looka da cat I gotta here," he beamed. And then began a discussion with Cedric as what to do with the kitten. Nobody knew what to do with it, and eventually Cedric asked me if I wanted the kitten. I said yes and took the cat home. I named my new friend Oliver Twist and referred to him as Olly. Olly grew into a beautiful big tom cat and would sleep on the end of my bed. I also had a magnificent huntsman spider which lived in my room for a couple years. Everyone else in the family was freaked out with the spider, but I loved it.

Unfortunately, being a tom, Olly would go out into the bush to hunt and fight with other cats and would sometimes come home the worse for wear. I would always leave my bedroom window open for him and he would come in and go straight to the end of the bed. I had a special bond with Olly, and cherished the time I had with that magnificent cat.

Now and again, Ingrid would have one of her girlfriends stay for the weekend. They were typical teenagers of that period, always preening, giggling, and talking girly shit. They were heavily into the music of the day also, particularly the Beatles, Tommy Roe, Steppenwolf, The Troggs, The Doors, The Stones, and so on. One afternoon I was lying on my bed with Olly and cleaning my air rifle, which Libby had bought for me on one of his trips to Perth. I was having a nice relaxing time with my cat and spider, but every now and then Ingrid and her friend would bounce into my room, give me a mouthful of crap and then exit, slamming the door on their way out. After the third time, I was starting to get jack of the pair of them and warned

Ingrid to not do it again. Well, golly gee, wouldn't you know it, they didn't listen and continued on.

I glanced at the cat and said something to the effect of: "I don't know about you, Olly, but I've had a gutsful of these two bitches." I got some silver paper, the sort you found wrapped around chocolate, and started to roll it into the shape of an air rifle pellet with a point on one end. After ten minutes I had a perfectly shaped pellet and inserted it into the barrel, cocked the gun, and waited. Sure enough, in they skipped; same crap, exited the room. But the exit on this occasion was vastly different from the others.

The friend was first to bounce out, closely followed by Ingrid. They both wore white tight-fitting shorts, skintight ones in fact. My room had one step into it and as Ingrid went onto the step, I lined up the right arse cheek and pow! The effect was instant. She jumped, screamed, grabbed her arse in a split second, and was gone. I heard the yelling and carry-on and the inevitable, "You wait until Mum gets home, you bastard." After 20 minutes or so, I ventured out of my room to see what the fall-out looked like. Ingrid was very unhappy, and when she turned around there was a little red circle resembling the Japanese flag on her nice white shorts. I couldn't help but laugh, and agreed with her that it would have stung a bit, but she should have listened when I told her to stop annoying me. Ingrid was pretty tough for a girl, and she got over it. I don't know whether she told Mum or not, but I never got into any trouble over the incident.

Cedric asked me if I wanted to earn some pocket money by ploughing a large paddock on the weekend. I jumped at the chance and said yes. The tractor was a Massey Ferguson 65, and the plough was a tandem disc type. Cedric set the depth of the plough and off I went. He told me the job would take two days, Saturday and Sunday. His estimation was spot on. Aubrey's mansion overlooked the paddock, and I could see a couple of people on the balcony, though not clearly as it was a reasonable distance away. I finished the job late Sunday afternoon and was pretty chuffed with the effort. Roughly a week went by, and I saw Jaimie Fowler. Jaimie took great delight in telling me I had ploughed his paddock too deeply and that I had ruined it and it would take years for it to recover. Apparently, he and Aubrey had been watching me through their binoculars. I was dumbfounded by this, and upset. I didn't say a word and just walked off. I never mentioned a word about it to anyone, not even Cedric.

During the harvest that year, 1968, Cedric got me to drive a grain truck in from the paddocks and unload it into the big grain shed, then go back out, and so on. Cedric taught me to be extremely careful when driving the truck as the load was massively heavy. I used to crawl along like a snail and didn't have a problem. Jaimie was operating the harvester and when he saw me driving the truck, I could tell he was not happy. The next day Aubrey went off his brain and told Cedric I was not allowed near any machinery whatsoever. Cedric told Aubrey that I was doing a very good job under his supervision and that I needed to learn just as Jaimie had learnt. The argument got heated and Cedric turned his back on Aubrey and walked back to the big shed. Cedric apologised to me and said how disappointed he was with Aubrey and his attitude. I didn't really know what to say, but I did thank Cedric for giving me a go. I started to really detest Aubrey, Jaimie and June Fowler with a vengeance. Aubrey and Jaimie only viewed me as a slave. I was good enough to pick mallee roots and rocks but not intelligent enough to operate machinery. I really wanted to punch the pair of them in the face, and my opportunity almost came with Jaimie a couple of years later.

At 16, I was doing Fourth Year high school and playing B Grade, with the odd 'A' grade game for Williams. Richard Fowler was playing B Grade also and would play the odd A Grade game too. I used to go over to Tommy Fowler's and have a kick in the paddock with Richard on a Saturday afternoon, as we would play on Sunday. Richard always encouraged me and made me strive to do better, particularly with kicking the footy. If I stuffed up a kick, he would be right onto me. He would let out a long sigh, hang onto the football and just look at me.

"Come on, Robert, you know you can do a lot better than that switch on, mate."

Richard would give me a lift to the footy and drop me home again. He was a Vietnam Vet and a hell of a good bloke. On the way home he would get stuck in the Williams pub for a few hours, and I would wander around or sit in the ute until he was ready to go. I didn't mind as I'd had plenty of practice waiting for Mum and Dad many times. On the way home we would talk about the game and Richard would often talk to me about Vietnam. I listened in awe but didn't know what to say really; but looking back, I now realise it didn't matter as he just needed to talk to someone about what went on over there, even if it was a 16-year-old kid. After listening to Richard, I always had so much respect and admiration for our Vietnam veterans. In my eyes they are all true heroes.

I'll never forget what Richard said to me out of the blue on the way to one of the games. He looked over to me and said, "Rob, you know, I really hope you go all the way with your footy, mate. I hope you play league football and one day play for Western Australia. I really believe you can do it." Once again, I was lost for words and just said something to the effect that I would love to do that.

I started to play more and more A Grade and got more confident with each game. I managed to dodge the hit merchants as I was too quick for them, and used my leap to enormous advantage, all the while getting stronger and more capable. Fourth Year high school was proving to be a waste of time. I was just not interested. There were five boys and about twenty-five girls in the class and this didn't help matters much. Academically, the five of us boys were reasonably ordinary and pretty much all pulled the pin (left) at the same time.

Another good mate of mine at high school was a kid called Rod Boehm. When I say he was a kid, that is far from the truth. Rod came to Narrogin High at fourteen years of age and was a very stocky and powerfully built lad. He was a good sportsman and we got on really well. Rodney was shaving at twelve and could have grown a full-on beard in a few weeks. Mum and Rodney's mother, May, became very good friends, and May would often drive out to the farm to spend some quality time with Maria. The pair of them didn't mind a drink or two and they had a lot of fun together. Rod would stay with us on school holidays, and it was on one of these occasions that Aubrey Fowler spotted him and in no time at all Aubrey had Rodney doing top dressing etc, just like one of his farm workers. Aubrey didn't offer me a job, so I was left to my own devices. Rod would be off at 7am and return at around 6pm, so I didn't get to see much of him at all during the school holidays.

Only a few of the subjects taught at high school would become useful or helpful in my adult life. The others were just rubbish and had little to do with equipping a young man on the arduous journey called life. I found maths, English, home economics and sport to be very useful, plus woodwork. I would come to use the knowledge gained from these subjects all the way through my adult life.

As far as I was concerned, algebra was something with stripes and was kept in a zoo; and the only use I got out of trigonometry was the pointy needle on the compass which I used to jab into an unsuspecting arse and gleefully wait for the reaction. We were all on the receiving end of that. Plus, there was a prank where a couple of drawing pins were poked through a ruler and you would position the ruler on the seat in front of you just as the recipient's bum was about to make contact with the seat. The reaction was always priceless. Mind you, once caught you would make sure it didn't happen again. I couldn't give a stuff about physics, chemistry, biology. And what the hell did I want to learn French for? After two years of study—I use that term loosely—I could only come up with one sentence: Il frappe Adolf avec une regle. What a waste of time. I would love to think that these days the education system concentrates more on preparing students for what lies ahead, rather than fill their heads with rubbish. I was more than happy to leave school.

2

INTO THE REAL WORLD AND A BOY'S DREAM

HALFWAY THROUGH FOURTH YEAR, I DECIDED TO LEAVE school and join the Bank of New South Wales in Narrogin. I was 16 and this was my first job. The first six months, I stayed at Rodney's place in town and would go home to the farm on weekends. Rod played footy for railways, and he organised for me to train with them during the week and then I would play for Williams on the weekend. Railways was coached by former Swan Districts champ Craig Noble. Rod introduced me to Craig, and I liked him as soon as we met. He had a nice personality, knew a lot about football, and treated me the same as his own players, even though I was the opposition. Unknown to me, Craig had been in contact with Swan Districts A League Football Club in Perth, and told them they had better come down and have a look at this kid.

I didn't mind working in the bank as everything at that stage of my life seemed exciting, especially earning a wage and playing football. May Boehm was starting to struggle a bit with her health, so I had to find alternative accommodation. Mum arranged for me to board at the Mardoch guest house, which was situated directly across the road from the Duke of York

Hotel. The Mardoch was a big building with a lot of rooms, and had a ground floor, first and second floors. I stayed in a room on the top floor. The place was a real eye opener for a young bloke like me. At times I felt like I was in the midst of One flew Over the Cuckoo's Nest, a movie depicting the antics of a group of nutters. One had to be nuts or totally insane to fit in here; but then all of a sudden you would find yourself sitting in the dining room with guys wearing suits, the complete opposite of the weirdos who stayed there. I kept to myself at the Mardoch but got to know all the clientele there and they just accepted me as one of the crowd.

I was having dinner in the dining room one night and found myself seated at a table with the Water Corporation fellows who had come down from Perth to do admin work. They were dressed immaculately and one of them was named Philip Glew. Phil had lost a key outside the Water Corp office and needed to find it. He stopped eating and glanced across at me.

"Look, mate. I need a set of good young eyes to find this bloody key. Can you give us a hand to find it?"

I tried to explain that my eyes were ordinary but decided to help anyway. We never found the key, but I chuckle when looking back. A future Fitzroy teammate of mine, Warwick Irwin, was to nickname me "Brail" for a good reason, and here I was using my "eagle eyes" to find a key in the dark. They may as well have gotten someone from the blind school; it would have been just as effective.

The lady who ran the Mardoch was Miss Byrne. She was in her fifties and a real eccentric. She had a right-hand man, Burly Bob, and to round out the trio, there was the Colonel. The Colonel had a monocle and army moustache, and spoke in clear matter-of-fact manner. He was doubly eccentric and looked to be around 80 years old. I was spellbound by the Colonel.

My room was situated directly above the local night club. The noise was horrific, and I felt I was right in the middle of the dance floor. Sleeping was becoming a huge problem for me. I decided to approach Burly Bob with my dilemma. Bob listened, then told me he wasn't sure if I could change rooms but to meet the trio in their sitting room at 8pm and they would see what could be done. I knocked and walked into the sitting room. Miss Byrne said, 'Hello, dear,' and asked me to sit down. I put my case forward and they all listened. After I had spoken, Miss Byrne looked at me with a concerned face and told me she wasn't sure what they could do at the moment, but she would give it some thought. She offered me a port, but I declined.

The Colonel looked as though he had already consumed a fair whack of port and he glanced over at me. He was smoking a cigar and the room was starting to get hazy from the smoke. The Colonel grabbed his monocle and planted it over his right eye. With yellow cigar-stained teeth he said, "Listen, son, the only advice I can give you is to look after your teeth." And with that the monocle dropped from his eye, he took another swig, and the meeting was over. Two weeks later I had a new room.

During this period, I met a young fellow who had been transferred from Perth to work in the bank at Narrogin. His name was Neil Shortte. Shorty and I would often go down to Narrogin oval and kick the footy around after work, then we would meet up for a milkshake at Berson's Garage which was located on Federal Street, up past Hordern Hotel, and made the best milkshakes in town. The milkshake containers were the old aluminum type, and they were ideal to drink a milkshake from. Shorty would always have spearmint and I would have chocolate.

Shorty grew up in Fremantle which is a port roughly 20 km from the city of Perth. It was established in 1829 and contains the heritage-listed Fremantle Jail. Freo was a tough place and Shorty came from a large family. We used to talk a lot and he told me that he had to leave home, because it was just too tough with all his brothers, and his father who ruled with an iron fist. He had to get out for his own safety and sanity. We became really good mates and Shorty loved football. He ended up playing for Imperials, whose colours were black and white. Imperials was one of the three Narrogin clubs, the other two being Towns and Railways. Shorty was a mad South Fremantle supporter and his brother Graeme played roughly 20 games of league football for Souths.

One Friday night it was getting a bit late, and Shorty boarded at a place about two kilometres from town. I had a spare bed in my room at the Mardoch, so rather than walk back to his place in the rain, he camped at the Mardoch for the night. Before we went to sleep, Shorty was talking about football and out of the blue he said, "I know you are going to make it big in football one day and when you do, I'm going to tell everyone I slept with Bobby Beecroft." We both had a good laugh and went to sleep. The 1968 footy season finished, and I turned my attention to cricket. I played for a Williams side called Country and was the youngest player in the side at 16 years of age.

Whilst working in the bank one day, I noticed a couple of gentlemen walk in around lunchtime. One had black slicked-back hair, a long black coat, white shirt, and a tie, and looked very fit; the other was more rotund and wore a sports jacket, white shirt, and tie. By this time, all the staff were staring at the two gentlemen and then I heard one of the staff members say, "Shit, that's Billy Walker." Bill Walker was a gun player for Swan Districts Football Club; and by "gun" I mean he was an out and out champion, one of the best players in Australia. The way the staff carried on you would have thought the Queen had just walked in.

Billy walked up to the counter and asked if young Robert Beecroft was around. I sure was. The next thing, I'm walking out the door with them. Billy had already seen the Manager, Fred Yull, and when we got outside, he asked if I knew a good place to get a milkshake. Well, I didn't need to think long and off we went to Bersen's Garage. The lady behind the counter already knew what flavour I would have and then we got down to talking. Billy started by saying Swans were keen to get me down to Bassendean, Swan Districts Football Club's home ground. Would I be interested? I don't know if I hid my excitement or not, but I was as keen as mustard to have a crack at league football. It had been my dream for years. He said Mum and Dad would have to sign a form tying me to Swans, which was a requirement of the West Australian Football League. They would have to sign on my behalf as I was only 17 years of age at the time. Billy also told me that the Club would be able to get me transferred from Narrogin to Perth with the Bank of New South Wales. I was over the moon and could hardly contain my excitement at the thought of going to the big time. This was to be the start of the dream I had held for years.

Not long after I had signed on with Swans, I was sitting in the grandstand at Williams Oval, waiting for my turn to bat. I was the only one sitting there. A fellow walked up the grandstand and sat right alongside me. "Are you Robert Beecroft?" he asked. I replied that I was and he told me his name was Mal

Atwell. All football followers knew who Mal Atwell was and I was no exception. Mal was a very tough and talented player and coach from the Perth Football Club. He told me that the Perth Football Club were very keen to get me to try out with them. I was a bit shocked and said I couldn't do that.

Mal gave me a stern look and said, "What do you mean you can't do that?"

I told him that Billy Walker had just signed me up to play with Swans Districts.

To say Mal was pissed off would be an understatement. He got up and let rip with, "That fucking little bastard!" And a couple of other adjectives were aimed at Billy. With that, he shook my hand and left.

On this particular day, we were playing Quindanning. This is a small town located between Williams and Boddington, approximately 160km from Perth. The town has a small population; in the 2006 census there were just 168 people. In the afternoon, players would take tea break for around 30 minutes and then play on until six o'clock. One of the Quindanning players was a fellow by the name of Donny Dowsett. Donny looked as though he had a mischievous streak in him. He was a bit of a larrikin, actually.

Donny decided tea was no good for him and belted up to the Williams pub for a quick beer. Play resumed and there was no sight of Donny. A sub was called onto the field to take his place. At around 5:30pm, Donny staggered onto the ground. He looked as though he'd been drinking rocket fuel for the few hours he had been missing. He had an ice cream cone with a huge vanilla scoop of ice cream sitting on top. Donny walked straight up to the bowler's end just before the start of a new over, and demanded the ball. The captain gave him the ball, as he knew there was no point in arguing with Donny right now. Donny bowled spin and in he came, ice cream in one hand and ball in the other. The first two balls missed the pitch, so Donny decided to let the umpire hold his ice cream, but not before he took a few licks. Our batsmen were running off the pitch to try and pat the ball back to Donny, just to get rid of him. In between balls, Donny would grab the ice cream from the umpire, give it a few licks and hand it back. By now the ice cream was melting profusely. The over seemed to take an eternity to complete and by the time it was finished, Donny had hair all over his face and ice cream from arsehole to breakfast time. Donny stumbled off the ground, got into his car and went straight back to the pub. Everyone breathed a sigh of relief and we got on with the game. That was the last time I saw Donny Dowsett, but I never forgot his antics on that day.

The 1969 football season came around and I knew it would be my last with Williams Football Club. By this time, I had attained my driver's licence and Dad lent me his car, an FB Holden which was blue and white. It wasn't long after this that Dad bought himself a Datsun 120Y so I had full use of the FB. I considered myself to be very lucky indeed. I had an outstanding football season for Williams in 1969 and won their Fairest and Best Award by a record margin.

It was halfway through the season that I met my first wife, Alicia. Alicia Kolenski was born on 11th December 1951 in the wheatbelt town of Merredin. Merredin is 260km east of Perth on the Great Eastern Highway and has a population of approximately 3500 people, very similar to but a little smaller than Narrogin. Alicia was nursing in Narrogin and stayed at the nurses' quarters which were situated next to the hospital. A friend of mine, Billy Rybarcyk, had teed up a blind date for me and it just so happened that the blind date was a nurse. Billy was going with a nurse called Jane, whom he later married, and at the time he thought this would be a good idea. Billy worked at Coles and had a bubbly personality; he drove a black Valiant and was a fun bloke to be around, so I agreed to the date.

Through Billy, I arranged to meet Alicia at one night during the week. I think it was a Wednesday as I had football training on Tuesdays and Thursdays. I went to the foyer of the nurses' quarters and waited a couple of minutes. As the girl came down the stairs, I knew it was Alicia from the description Billy had given me. She was 170-175cm tall, had beautiful hair and was very good looking. I was taken by her lovely smile and stunning brown eyes. She said, "Hi, I'm Alicia. Are you Robert?" And that was it. I took her hand and walked to the car and then drove to where else but Bersen's Garage for, you guessed it, a milkshake.

We hit it off straight away and talked for a few hours. I was captivated by this girl and started seeing Alicia fairly often as the weeks passed. She had a wonderful personality, and it wasn't long before I felt a very strong attraction to her, and it was clear Alicia felt the same way about me. I took her home to meet Mum and Dad and we stayed on the farm for the weekend. Mum and Dad liked her, so everything was good.

Ingrid at this stage was working in Perth for Marsden's Plumbing, her first job. So Alicia slept in her room, which was located next to Mum and Dad. During the night, Alicia snuck into my room and slept the night with me. We weren't having sex at that stage, but Mum was not happy that Alicia had ended up in my bed.

Mum got hold of me the next day on my own and said, "I knew dat little bitch get in your room. You not let ker in again."

The old woman was right onto it, so I let Alicia know and she understood. A few weeks after this, we started having sex. I went to Merredin with Alicia to meet the family. Her father, Ignacey Kolenski, was Polish, and his wife, Elsa, was Russian, Alicia had two younger sisters, Heather and Jean, and one older sister, Renae. There was also one younger brother, Troy. Ignacey was extremely intelligent, a gifted artist, and a gun welder as well, and he worked for the water supply in Merredin. Elsa was a lovely lady who was always organised and had a warm, friendly personality. Ignacey could do anything, but his flaw was drinking and smoking. He did both to excess. He had been through the war and had also spent time in the coal mines, which affected his lungs badly. Looking back, I can't say I blame him for his addictions. Some of his stories were quite horrific.

I got on very well with Alicia's family, but there was only one thing I desperately wanted to do and that was to get to Perth and play league football. In December of 1969 I was getting ready to move down to Perth. Swans had arranged a transfer to the Mount Lawley Branch of the bank, and I was to be down there ready to start preseason training in early January. Alicia was hell bent on getting a transfer to St John of God Hospital in Subiaco, so that she could join me in Perth. I told her not to follow me to Perth, as my priority was football and only football. I told her several times, "Please don't follow me to Perth. I need to put everything into football. It's my dream and I'm going to give it 100%." I may as well have been talking to a brick wall, as it did not register.

I moved to Perth and stayed the first few months with my Aunty Lorna, who lived in Sabina Street, Mount Lawley. Preseason got under way with a long slog along the beach at Scarborough. There were 60-70 players there all trying to have a crack at league football. I looked around and recognised players I had seen on television, and here I was with them: Peter Manning, Stan Nowotny, Lou Milanko, John O'Neil, Barry Stockden, Billy Walker, of course, and a few others. Swans then arranged accommodation for me with Mr and Mrs Wilson in Morley. Gordon Wilson was the caretaker at Hampton High School and their house was on the school grounds. I boarded with them for about nine months.

Preseason was going along really well, and I was full of beans, heaps of energy and looking forward to the practice matches in March/April. I would go home every couple of weekends and at these times I would see Alicia. On one of these trips, Alicia said she had gotten a transfer to St John of God Hospital. I explained that with footy I wouldn't have a lot of time with her, and again said my sole focus would be football. Alicia said she completely understood but she wanted to be near me, and it wouldn't interfere with my football.

I said, "Well, I've told you, so if you are okay with that then I guess it's fine." Very soon after this, Alicia was down at St John of God Hospital in Subiaco.

The practice matches had finally arrived, and I couldn't wait to get into it. The first practice match was an intra-club affair and I was given a Perth jumper number 10 to wear. I started in a forward pocket and had a few runs in the ruck. In the first 10 minutes I leapt on top of a pack of players and took a big grab then went back and slotted a goal. When it was my turn in ruck, I relished the opportunity to bound around the ground, taking big marks and leaping high in the centre bounces. I had come from playing on hard grounds, and here I was running around on a carpet of green grass; oh boy, how good was this.

All the practice matches went well for me, and the talk was that I could find myself in the league side for the opener at East Fremantle Oval to take on the very strong East Fremantle side. I would just have to wait and see.

One of the memories that has stuck in my mind from the early practice matches was playing on a team mate who went by the nick name of Bear. Bear was trying to establish himself, as we all were, and desperately wanted to crack a league game. While resting in the forward line I jumped on his shoulders twice in the space of five minutes and took two screamers, kicking a goal after each.

Bear turned to me and blurted, "Listen, mate, you have ruined my fucking career in five minutes. Why don't you just fuck off and go play in the ruck."

Well, what could I say but: "Sorry, mate."

He looked at me and added, "Look, I can tell you will be around for a long time, 10-15 years. Me, I just want to play a couple of league games, so please go play on the ball." I had a laugh. It was time to have another run in the ruck anyway.

I was seeing Alicia regularly and she came to all the practice matches. One particular night, Alicia decided to stay overnight and slept in my room while I was boarding with the Wilsons. Gordon didn't take too kindly to this and carried on like a pork chop. He wanted me out and I was only too happy to oblige. I liked Mrs Wilson a lot and got on very well with her, but Gordon was a real pain in the arse. He was a boring little bespectacled control freak. There wasn't one single thing I liked about the person. I remember having a kick of the footy on the Hampton High School grounds near the caretaker's cottage, where the Wilsons lived. We were doing kick to kick, with my two good mates Max George and Greg Murray, both

Swans boys like myself. We had been going about two minutes when out stormed Gordon. He carried on like a little gestapo and told us to get off the school grounds.

He shrieked, "Get off! I don't allow anyone on these grounds outside of school hours."

Greg Murray, who was a schoolteacher himself, glanced over and said to Gordon, "Are you serious?"

By this time, Gordon was in a real fluster and just screamed, "Get off, get off now!"

I grabbed Greg by the arm, looked at Wilson, and said, "Come on, mate, don't argue with the fuckwit."

My relationship with Gordon only went downhill from there. I had arranged to rent a flat in Midland just off Railway Parade but had to wait a week for things to be finalised. Alicia would be moving in with me.

Just before the sleep-over incident, Alicia was sitting in the car with me outside the St John of God Hospital, where she worked. She was beaming and explained that she had some exciting news for me. I wondered what the hell this exciting news could possibly be. Alicia then gushed, "I'm pregnant." The shock for me was instant. It was as if a bolt of lightning had struck me. I knew right there and then that my life was going to change for the worse. Alicia was on the pill – how the hell had this happened? I put my head in my hands and just sobbed. Here I was, 18 years old, and now I had this to contend with. Alicia thought I would be elated and didn't expect the reaction that she got. I asked how this could happen, and as usual she had a story. I never questioned Alicia, and that would continue for many, many years.

After getting over the shock of it all, we both moved into the flat and got on with life. We decided to get married in

December, after the football season. In those days if you got a girl pregnant, you married her and took on the responsibility. Looking back, I wished to God that I could have kept my dick in my pants. This was my fault and I now had to take care of the situation, even as an 18-year-old. The families had to be told and that would be another challenge. We decided not to tell them until a few months had passed. This was only early days and I had to ready myself for my first season in league football.

Two huge challenges lay ahead of me and needed to be taken head on. The 1970 League football season had finally arrived. The preseason, like all preseason training, had been hard; but I got through it and was ready to go. I still wasn't sure if I would be selected in the league side for the first game, but I was confident as my form had been very good. The team was finally selected, and my name was read out. I was to start in the ruck, right in the thick of it, in the middle of East Fremantle Oval for the first bounce.

Trying to contain the excitement was hopeless. My dream had finally arrived and now the rest was up to me. On match day the butterflies in my stomach were running rampant. I was so nervous I felt like vomiting. When I got to the ground, I actually paid to get in, not realising players were issued with a pass but apparently someone had forgotten to give me one. The boys had a good old laugh about it, saying stuff like, "Hey, Bumbles," (my nickname), "they pay to watch you. You don't pay to play! Welcome to league football, mate."

3
ECSTASY AND TORMENT

WE RAN OUT ONTO THE GROUND AND THE FEELING WAS euphoric. I felt great at the start of the game. I lined up opposite Brian "The Whale" Roberts, ready for the first bounce and ready for battle. The Whale was a South Australian State player and a man mountain. He stood approximately 200cm tall and weighed 120kg. He was to go on and play in the VFL with Richmond under the legendary Tommy Hafey. The Whale must have been licking his lips, looking at this skinny kid on the other side of the circle. But he was to get the shock of his life, as I continually jumped over the top of him and had a good game. At the end of the game, Swans had been soundly beaten and I ended up in the best players list.

I played every game in my first year and won the League's Best First Year Player award, as well as a brand spanking new Datsun car. Datcenter Midland had donated the car to the club, and it was to be presented to the best player at the end of the season. I gave myself no chance whatsoever as far as winning the car went. I just got on with my footy. The club used a handicap system to make it fair for all players, including the experienced champions right down to a first-year player like me. Because I had played every game and had a good season, I was lucky enough to win this magnificent prize. I ended up finishing fourth in the Fairest and Best in 1970. I was very happy with my first year in league football.

Alicia had given away nursing and was working in a friend's boutique which sold clothes amongst other things. She had gone to school with this friend. I got a call from Billy one day and he wanted to talk to me about something. Billy picked me up and we went for a drive in his car. He pulled up and told me he'd had a call from a woman who accused Alicia of stealing clothes and things from her shop. I told him I didn't know anything about this, but knew Alicia had been working in a shop. Billy went on to say the Club could arrange help for Alicia if she was having problems. I told him I didn't think she had any problems at all, and that was it.

A few weeks after the meeting with Billy, Alicia and I were lying in bed. It was around 6am and I had just woken up. Suddenly there was banging and shouting at the door. I jumped out of bed and opened the door, and to my horror five or six men in suits stormed in. They were detectives. They produced a warrant and began searching the place. One of them started pulling new clothes boxes and even a sewing machine out from under the bed. As well as being shocked, I was also dumbfounded at what I saw. I had never even looked under the bed and now I was staring at all this. All of it was stolen goods.

The detectives arrested Alicia and took her away. I felt so ashamed and just sat on the bed, completely numb. I met Ignacey and Elsa at the East Perth lockup that afternoon. Alicia was out on bail and her parents wanted to know what was going on. Alicia claimed that all the stuff was given to her in lieu of wages and she didn't steal anything—another story which I believed. Her friend's mother, who owned the shop, was happy to get all the goods back and subsequently dropped the charges.

We decided to get married on December 4th, 1970, and we tied the knot with Alicia about five or six months pregnant. Had Alicia not been pregnant, I would never have gone with her again, let alone have got married to her. I felt trapped into the marriage and that feeling never left me.

Just after the wedding we moved into an old house in Greenmount. The house was at the top of Greenmount Hill, near the Bilgoman pool, just off Waylan Avenue. The rent was $12 per week and even that seemed too much. The bathroom had a huge hole in the wall, right over the bath. The water was heated by a wood chip heater and when you sat in the bath, the wind would howl through the hole. The rest of the place was livable, though only just; but that's all we could afford at the time.

I threw myself into training and had mapped out a tough six-kilometre run through the hills, which I did four times a week. As well as doing the Swans preseason, I kept these runs going, plus I was doing hundreds of push-ups and weights with rocks. My legs got bigger and stronger, particularly my calf muscles, and my upper body was getting stronger as well. I was very determined to make my mark in league football. The 1971 preseason was going well, and I felt fitter and stronger than ever.

On the 24th of March 1971, Tanya Nicole Beecroft was born at the Swan Districts Hospital Midland. I looked at this beautiful little girl and realised she was my responsibility, and knew I would always protect her and look after her. It felt strange, though, being a father at nineteen years of age. Alicia was thrilled to bits and turned out to be a super mother, as most mothers are. They don't get the accolades they deserve. In my eyes, good mothers are the true heroes.

We travelled down to the farm and stayed with Mum and Dad now and again. During one of these stays, my Uncle Bob was visiting, and he had brought one of my cousins along. Mum had cooked a roast and we were about to eat. We were all seated around the kitchen table. It was raining and Mum remarked that there was bread and some mail in the letter box, which was situated on the main road about 40 metres from the house. Alicia told Mum that she would collect it and asked Dad if she could drive out onto the main road, collect the bread and mail, then drive back.

We then all settled in for a nice lunch. All of a sudden, there was a very loud banging on the door. The door opened into the kitchen. Mum opened the door and there was Jaimie Fowler. He started getting stuck into Alicia and told her she was not to drive the ute under any circumstances. He had really raised his voice and was pointing his finger at her. My family were gobsmacked and didn't say a word. As usual, Jaimie had been watching the house through his binoculars; whether it was from the top sheds or from his own balcony, I don't know.

I jumped up from the table and sent my chair flying, trying to get to Jaimie. By the time I got to the door, he had bolted. I tore after him, but he just beat me to his ute which was on the main road. He jumped in and locked his door. Jaimie's wife Jo was in the car.

She wound her window down and said, "Robert, I thought you were a nice boy. I've been told you were a nice boy." She communicated this in a sarcastic manner.

"Shut up, you fucking stupid bitch," I told her. I looked through the window at Jaimie and said to him, "If you ever come to this house while I'm here, I will smash the fuck out of you. Now fuck off, you cowardly punce." I never had any more problems from Jaimie Fowler or any of them.

I went back into the kitchen and Uncle Bob looked at me with a big grin on his face.

"Did you give the bastard a flogging?" he asked.

"Almost, Uncle Bob," I replied. Then we all had a good laugh and got on with lunch.

By this stage I had been transferred to Midland with the bank, so I could be closer to Bassendean and get to training more easily. The bank job was wearing thin with me, as it was hard to get away on time for training, especially if you had a smart-arse accountant that liked his little power trip. Anyway, I stuck it out for now.

One of my teammates was a fellow named John Rose, a big strapping bloke who had started at Swans the same time as me. I dropped into Johnny's place. He lived with his mum and dad on Great Northern Hwy, about a kilometre from the centre of Midland.

When I got there, John said, "While you're here, mate, come and meet Pops."

I walked around to the front verandah and John introduced me to his pop. He was a man in his late seventies with a strong, determined face and a wiry but strong build. He reached out and shook my hand and said, "G'day." And that was about it. I had just met Bert Facey, famous for his book A Fortunate life. John Rose was his grandson, and he was the one who had organised for the book to be written after going through Bert's old exercise books where he had kept a record of his hard life.

It would be ten years, 1981, before the book was published, and only nine months before Bert Facey's death.

During the summer of 1971, my sister Ingrid and her husband, Jeff, visited and we had a meal and a few beers. There was also another couple there. At about 8pm there was a knock on the door. I opened the door and there were two policemen standing there. They told me that the lady next door had accused Alicia of stealing her purse and although they didn't have a warrant, they asked if they could have a quick look around. I said okay, but not to go into the lounge, as I had people over. They agreed.

They went into the bathroom and opened the chip heater and there it was, a brown purse. I was horrified. Here we go again. The woman didn't go on with any charge, but never had anything to do with Alicia again. Alicia came up with some cock and bull story and I believed her. I didn't want to believe anything else and put the saga into the back of my mind.

A couple of days later, the police were at the house again, but this time my teammate Darryl Balchin was with them. Dags was a big burly ruckman who had taken me under his wing at Swans, and he was a guy I respected and really liked. He was a copper and would eventually rise to be a Chief Inspector in the WA Police Force.

Dags asked me what was going on with Alicia. "Is she short of money? Does she have a problem? Mate," he said, "there are easier ways to make money than what she is doing. You need to have a good talk to her."

"Okay, mate," I said. "I'll see you at the training." And off they went.

I felt a wave of shame and embarrassment wash over me. I didn't deserve this, but I had to stick with Alicia because I had a little girl to take care of now. I got lost in my training and really flogged myself. It took my mind off everything else.

The 1971 season was fast approaching, and I was as ready as I could be, waiting eagerly for the season to get underway. I was having trouble with my eyes and the Club arranged for me to see an eye specialist to have contact lenses made. Because I had such bad stigmatisms in each eye, contact lenses were extremely hard to fit. The specialist persisted and I had the lenses made. They were okay, not perfect by any means, but better than nothing. Every now and again one would come out and get lost, particularly if I copped a whack in the face; but after this happened a couple of times, I had a spare set made. I got by.

The 1971 season came and went. Once again, I played every game and finished fourth in the club Fairest and Best count. I was happy with the way I played and was now starting to feel very comfortable with league football. In fact, I started to feel a part of it. My next goal was to play State football, and I set my mind on this. I did a lot of training away from Bassendean, extra training that I thought I needed to do. The determination to play for WA drove me.

We were still living in the Greenmount house and Alicia was fully engrossed with Tanya. Everything was settled and Alicia appeared to be happy and content. She was an exceptionally good mother and looked as though she had been looking after children all her life. Alicia and I were lying in bed one night at about 10pm. We heard a loud knock at the door, almost a banging. I jumped up and put track pants on and grabbed a large butcher's knife from the kitchen then pulled open the door.

The bloke at the door stepped back quickly and yelled out, "Fuck, mate, it's only me! Put the knife away!"

I immediately recognised him. It was Gary Bowden, a mate I worked with at the bank. He had four long necks— large bottles of beer—and nearly dropped the lot.

"What the fuck's with the big knife, mate? I thought you were going to kill me." Old Gazza was pretty shaken up.

I just smiled and said, "You never know who's at the door this time of night up here. Come in, Gazza."

Now and again, Gary would get on the wallop and just appear. On this occasion he had caught a taxi up. I had a coffee while he drank beer, and Alicia made a bed for him on the lounge. We all then retired for the night.

The 1972 season was just around the corner, and I felt stronger and fitter than I had ever been. It had been the hardest preseason I had put in so far. With the extra work and Swans solid preseason, I was well and truly primed. The summer had also seen a change of coach at Swans. Billy Walker had been at the helm for two years and through no fault of his, we had won only a few games.

Jack Ensor was appointed as coach, and I spent four good years under Jack. Jack had a disarming personality and was a student of the game. He had been invaluable to both Mal Atwell and Ken Armstrong at the Perth Football Club and now he had his own side. Billy stayed on as a player and captain. The season got underway, and the team showed improvement under Jack.

My form was very good, and I was able to maintain it week in and week out. Everything had come together. In those days there used to be a carnival played between the States once every three years, and this year, 1972, it was WA's turn to host the carnival at Subiaco oval on June 17th. The State squad was announced a couple of months before the carnival, and I was over the moon when my name came up.

The side was to be coached by the legendary Haydn Bunton Jnr., and would get together for training every Monday, which would be increased as the carnival got closer. Bunts was a great guy and had a very likeable demeanour, and he knew football inside out. Every Monday he would remind us all that we had to keep our form up or we would be replaced. I looked around me and there were champions everywhere: Mal Brown, Barry Cable, Colin Tully, George Young, Graham Moss, Mike Fitzpatrick, Peter Steward, Dennis Marshall, and the list went on. I found it hard to believe I was there.

Well, believe it or not, I was there and now I had to seize my opportunity with both hands. I was the only player chosen from Swan Districts and felt immensely proud. My form stuck with me, and I was having a standout season. A couple of weeks out from the carnival, Bunts pulled me aside and told me I would be leading the rucks for WA. He told me to make sure I held my form over the next two weeks. I was elated. Bunts had put me in front of Graham Moss and Mike Fitzpatrick, and I desperately wanted to repay his faith in me.

My form held over the next two weeks, and I was named first ruck to play on the Saturday against South Australia. I was a bag of nerves during the week, so I went and saw Keith Slater up in Greenmount. Spud was a WA sporting legend who had played in Swans Premiership sides in the early sixties, and had also played Test Cricket for Australia. He had a huge welcoming smile that would light up a room. I sat with Spudda, as I called him, for about two hours.

Just before I left, he fixed a gaze on me and began, "Look, if you get a free kick in the middle early, don't muck around. Go back and drill a big screwie," (torpedo punt kick) "as far and as hard as you can towards the goal square. It will lift you and everyone else." I thanked Spud for his time and felt a lot more settled. I was ready for the biggest challenge in my football life.

Saturday, June 17th, 1972, came around finally. Here I was, lined up with my WA teammates and looking straight across at the South Australian boys lined up opposite us. The game would be in a few minutes. The only thing on my mind at that moment was how desperately I wanted to tear those blokes apart, and I guess most of them felt like me.

Looking across, I could see Russell Ebert, Paul Bagshaw, Barry Robran, Adcock, Phillis, and so on. All champion South Aussie footballers. And there were also a few who would go on to make their mark in football, including Graeme Cornes and Malcom Blight. Also standing towards one end of that line was John Wynne, an ex-West Aussie who had gone over to South Australia to play with Norwood. This side was riddled with stars, but they all had two arms and two legs just like me.

The game got under way, and I flew into my work in the middle. Full of adrenaline, I leapt like never before. Very early on, I received a free kick, right in the centre of Subiaco oval. It was surreal. I heard Spud's words ringing through my head. I had no hesitation and went back and drove a huge screwie to the front of the goal square. It came off the boot so sweetly and barrelled through the air like a rocket. I felt fantastic and was transfixed by what had just happened.

Not long after this, I sprinted across to the southern wing, as WA had won possession on the half back flank and a long kick up the line was on its way. Peter Marker, the South Australian captain, got there ten metres before me and as the ball came down the wing, I jumped on top of him and took a screamer, then went back and drove a drop kick deep into our forward line.

I was having a cracker of a game, but just before half time, South Aussie Ruckman Dean Ottens (father of Brad Ottens – the Richmond and Geelong champ), threw a vicious forearm back and opened a big gash just under my chin. Blood squirted all over the front of my jumper. Trainers put a thick large band-aid over the wound and then the half time siren went. The doctor grabbed me as soon as I entered the rooms, and next thing, I'm on my back looking up at him.

"Well, son, we don't have time for an anaesthetic. Do you think you'll be okay? I need to put half a dozen stitches in. Yell out if it gets to be too much."

With that, he started to stitch the wound and it was all over pretty quickly. I could feel the needle doing its work, but I was on a real high and felt little pain at all. At the end of the game, WA had won by eight or nine goals and I was named amongst the best for WA. Wow, what an introduction to State football. My dreams had all come true.

The next game was against Tasmania on Wednesday, and it came around very quickly with only a one-day break. The game against Tasmania was underway and I got off to a flyer. After a solid fifteen minutes on the ball, I went down to the forward pocket for a spell. In the next ten to fifteen minutes, I had kicked four goals and we took a five-goal lead into half time. WA's form continued and at the end we had won by 45 points, another solid victory. I had a very good game and was named in the Best Players list again.

The last game of the carnival was to be held on Saturday against the all-conquering Victorians, a side full of out and out champions including John Nicholls, Leigh Matthews, Keith Greig, Alex Jesaulinko, Len Thompson, Peter McKenna; and the list went on. My opponents on the day would be Len

Thompson, John Nicholls and Gary Dempsey, a very daunting trio indeed. Like all opponents, I acknowledged the fact they were there and respected them; other than that, I didn't give a damn about who they were.

On Saturday it was game on, and Subiaco was bursting at the seams. The game unfolded and it was a torrid affair. The Vics were all strong and the pressure was on all over the ground, but we held our own against them and by three-quarter time we were only three goals down. I really felt we could win this one, but unfortunately by game's end WA went down by 44 points. I enjoyed the type of footy the Vics played—unrelenting and very physical. The game set the fire in my belly to one-day play in the VFL, the best and toughest competition in Australia.

I was sitting in the change rooms after the game and just taking it all in. I'd had a very good carnival and was very pleased about it all. We had been there for approximately ten minutes when Mal Brown plonked himself alongside me.

"Hey, you little bastard, you're in," he gushed.

"In what, Browney?" I asked.

"In the bloody All-Australian side, mate."

Boy, I couldn't believe it. I'd played my first State football and was now in the All-Australian team. The whole thing took a while to process.

Mum and Dad, plus my sister Ingrid, had come down to watch the carnival. In fact, the game against South Australia was the first time Dad had ever seen me play. Dad never used to say a lot, but he was as proud as punch after the game, as were Mum and Ingrid. I wondered if Dad ever remembered my words to him at that final between Perth and East Perth. It's something I never brought up with him, but I would like to think that he did.

Now the carnival was over, it was back to finishing off the season with Swans. I rocked up to the training on Tuesday and was congratulated by Jack and all my teammates.

Jack then turned his attention to me and said, "Now, Bob, you have played three games in one week. What are you doing here?"

"I'm here to train, Jack," I said sheepishly.

"No, you're not, young man. I think you've done enough training over the past week. Now off you go and have a rest."

"No, I'll be okay, Jack," I replied.

"No. Off you go. I will see you on Thursday." So off I went and had a night off from training.

We played the season out and the Swans had won seven games for the year. A good improvement on the previous season. At the beginning of August, three gentlemen pulled up outside the house, and the one who spoke was George Harris, the no-nonsense head of the Carlton Football Club.

"You have been selected to tour with the All-Stars team to London on the 22nd of October this year. We will be playing an exhibition game at the oval in London, one in Greece, and another in Singapore on the way home. You will tour with and play against Carlton. You will receive all necessary correspondence in due course. Make sure you get a passport."

I asked George if he would like a coffee, as this meeting had taken place outside the front door.

"No thank you. I'll see you in Melbourne," he replied, and off they went.

Momentarily, I wondered what George thought of the crap house I was living in; but then the woosh of excitement took over and I needed to gather my thoughts. I had never been on a plane, or even out of the State before, and here I was about to fly all the way to London. I needed to tell Alicia and then sit down. Things were happening way too fast.

I attended the Swan Medal Count at season's end and wound up winning the Swan medal for the Best Player in 1972. Not long after this, I approached the General Manager of Swans, Stan Moses, a man I could not stand. I told him I was sick of living in a shit hole up in Greenmount and wanted the Club to pay rent on a decent house for me. Moses turned scarlet and told me not to get carried away with myself and that a lot of people around the Club didn't think I deserved to be in the All-Australian side. I looked the prick in the eye and told him if the Club didn't pay my rent, I would not be playing footy with Swans. I got up and walked out.

A week later, Moses called me into his office and said the Club would pay my rent and to make sure I didn't tell anyone. Moses was the same man who wrote his own ten-year contract with the Club and thought he owned the place. Within a couple of weeks, I moved my family into Lot 4, Victoria Parade, Midvale. It was a huge improvement on the Greenmount house even though the rent wasn't significantly higher. Besides reasonably low match fees, this was the only thing that I ever received from the Club in my six years with them. Swans set up what they called a provident fund for all league players. They put money into your fund after each league game. By the time I left Swans, I had around $5,000 in the fund, but was never to see one red cent of it.

Moses had come up with a Swan Districts postcard, which was an aerial shot of Bassendean with my picture on the right-hand side of the card. He never asked my permission to be used in this way. In fact, he never even discussed it with me, and this was after telling me I shouldn't have been in the All-Australian team. Years later, Moses tried to make peace with me by way of a letter. I just ripped it up and threw it in the bin.

The Club had put a ban on any scouts from Victoria talking to me. There were headlines in the West Australian newspaper saying how a few clubs in Victoria were very interested in speaking to me with the view of playing in the VFL. I was a teller at the bank in Midland by this stage, and one day I was approached by a well-dressed gentleman who walked up to the counter at the bank and said, "Hi, Bob, my name is Bruce Wilkinson, and I am the Secretary of the Fitzroy Football Club. What time do you go to lunch?"

Bruce and I had lunch at the Council Club Hotel in Midland, and the discussion started. He showed me a contract for between $6,000 and $7,000, and explained that if I was prepared to sign today, he would write out a cheque for $1,200 on the spot. I was only earning between five and six grand a year in the bank, so I jumped at the chance. I signed, Bruce gave me a cheque, and the meeting was over. As we parted, Bruce told me it was going to be a battle to get me away from Swans, but I had to keep pushing. They wanted me over in Melbourne as soon as possible. Well, Bruce was right; it was going to be a battle royale.

When the Club got wind of what had taken place, as expected, Moses was furious. He raved on about how much it had cost the Club to develop me (I'd love to see the invoice for that one) and said that I wouldn't be cleared to Fitzroy or anywhere else under any circumstances. A week later, I was in Moses' office again, but this time butter wouldn't even melt in Stanley's mouth.

"Look, mate, just give us two good years and the Club will clear you. We know how much you would like to play in the VFL and prove yourself over there."

I thought it was reasonable and didn't ask for anything. I just wanted to get the two years done and head to the big time.

Now it was time to prepare for the trip of a lifetime, the trip to Europe with the All-Stars team. I applied for a passport and was issued one on the 8th of August 1972. The trip would last just over three weeks, and all players were to be given $500 spending money, uniforms, footy jumpers, etc. We would leave from Melbourne at 1850 hours on the 22nd October, stop to refuel at Singapore, and then arrive in London at 1030 hours on 23rd October.

Just before I left Perth to fly to Melbourne, my family gathered to say goodbye. Mum was really worried about her little boy, and I remember her going up to Mal Brown and saying, "Melcum, you mek sure you look arpta my boy." Browny gave her a cheeky smile and beamed at her, saying, "Don't you worry about a thing, Mrs Beecroft, I'll take good care of your boy." And with that we were on our way.

Everything about the trip was exciting, especially for a young bloke like me who had never been out of WA. I was blown away by the history and size of London and all the other places—Holland, Paris, Scotland, Athens, Singapore—and found it difficult to take everything in. The fact that we were drinking every day didn't help much either.

We played an exhibition game at the oval in London, where the players got to meet with Prince Charles and the Duke of Edinburgh. The Adventures of Barry McKenzie was being filmed in London at the time, and Barry Crocker was there as he was a good Carlton fan. There were approximately 12,000 people at the game. The pitches were all covered by red matting to protect them during play. The game was close, with Carlton running out winners by one goal. There was some good football played and the crowd enjoyed it.

In all there were three games played, the next one in Greece, and the final one in Singapore. The ground in Greece was rock hard and the game drew a crowd of 3,000, and the All-Stars triumphed 127-124. In Singapore the hot humid conditions were extremely oppressive and by game's end, the All-Stars triumphed once again at 77 to 65 in front of 8,500 spectators.

Towards the end of the trip, I was keen to get home as I was missing Alicia and Tanya and had enough of the travelling and constant drinking. The trip was a once-in-a-lifetime experience and one I won't ever forget. It was good to get home and settle into a normal life again, but it took a while to come down mentally from the extraordinary trip to Europe.

4
MORE OF LIFE'S LESSONS

TIME WENT QUICKLY AND IT WASN'T LONG BEFORE WE WERE back into preseason training for the upcoming 1973 season. 1973 was to become my biggest lesson in football, and life in general. Mentally I thought, Well, I've gone to the top of the mountain; it will all just happen for me from now on. What a huge mistake. All of a sudden, I didn't put in the extra work, the extra hard yards that got me to the top of the tree. Everything had happened very quickly for me, and my head was not in the right space for the super-competitive and brutal world of league football. I struggled through the practice games and a few of the early games of 1973. I just wasn't where I should have been.

Jack Ensor, our coach, told me my form was terrible and I agreed with him. He told me I would be on the bench, reserve, in Saturday's match. Swans struggled that day and Jack left me on the bench for three-quarters of the game. I came on for the last quarter and played extremely well. We ended up going down narrowly, but I couldn't have been happier with my quarter of football.

Swans champ Peter Manning came up to me and said, "It's a bloody absolute disgrace what Ensor did today, mate. We would have won today if you had played the whole game. I'm disgusted." I told Pete it was my own fault I was on the bench and not to worry about it.

Funnily enough, it was the wake-up call I needed, and Jack was right to do what he did that day. At season's end, Swans had won eight games and improved on the previous year's performance. I finished sixth in the Fairest and Best award which wasn't a bad effort, considering the start I had. I had also learnt a big lesson which I would never ever forget.

I started training for the 1974 season in early October, a couple of months earlier than normal. I was back running my Greenmount hill run and doing more upper body work. Once a week I would train at the Helena Valley Racetrack. I was doing five days a week and the determination was sky high. By mid-December I was in the best shape ever, heading into the Club's official preseason.

One Friday night I decided to go to the pub with a few of my workmates from the bank. It was towards the end of December, and I had been training like a trojan so decided to go with them and have a night off training. We all wandered over the road to the Junction Hotel, which is opposite the Town Hall in Midland. The hotel has a different name today. By this stage, Alicia and I had also moved into another house, at 1 Swan Street, Middle Swan.

The pub shut at 10pm and I was walking down towards Railway Parade with my workmate Kevin West. Westy was around 178cm tall and was very thin. He was a good bloke with a top personality. We were walking towards our cars and had only gone 20 metres when a car screamed up and one of the occupants asked where they could get a beer this time of night. I told them maybe at Bruce Cale's pub just around the corner, as Brucey was known to sell grog right up to the death knell and they might be lucky.

They were back in no time at all. Westy and I had only gone about a hundred metres at this point. There were five of them in the car and the fellow in the front passenger seat started abusing Westy and me for bullshitting. Then all but one of them got out of the car and formed a ring around me. Westy had moved back against a shop wall, and I could see he was terrified. The punks surrounding me were all relatively short and they all had their arms folded.

I looked the mouthy one in the eye and said, "What do you fucking little monkeys want?"

He looked surprised that I wasn't scared of them and boasted that they had a bloke in the car that would well and truly shut my big mouth. I looked over at Westy and he was visibly shaken. I then took my glasses off and threw them over to Westy and told him to hang onto them. At this point, the punks all stepped away to one side and a big fellow got out of the car. He was roughly 180cm tall with a solid build, and long wavy dark hair which was just over shoulder length. He had a starchy long-sleeved shirt on, with the sleeves rolled up towards his elbows, and rings on his fingers.

I fixed my eyes onto him, and he walked straight up to me. He immediately threw a right and I could hear his starchy shirt move before his fist reached me. I moved my head to the left and the blow grazed the right side of my face and as that happened, I grabbed his hair with my left hand and delivered about a dozen huge uppercuts straight into his face. I could feel all the energy go out of his body, then I drove another half dozen into him. All of a sudden, he collapsed into the gutter, ripping every button off my shirt as he went down. I stood there and looked at him and then he tried to get up. I told him to stay in the gutter where he belonged, or I would finish him completely. He didn't listen and got up onto one knee, so I let go with a huge punch that laid him flat. He was finished fighting.

At that point I looked across at the little cowards and that's when one of them said, "Fuck, we know who you are. You're Bobby Beecroft, and you play for Swans Districts."

I walked over to him, and he literally shat himself as I looked him right in the eye and fumed, "Yes, you little cunt, and you and your cowardly mates will remember this night for the rest of your lives. If I ever see any of you punks anywhere, this is how you will end up. Now, take that piece of shit out of the gutter and put it in your car."

The fellow in the gutter was covered in blood and his face looked like it had been through a mincer. The punks were in complete shock and didn't say a word. My shirt was covered in the aggressor's blood, and it didn't have any buttons left on the front, so I took it off and threw it in the gutter with the meathead.

"Come on Westy, let's go," I said.

Well, poor old Westy was shaking so I told him to follow me home so he could settle down a bit.

Once we were home, Alicia opened the door and said, "What the fuck have you been doing?"

Westy blurted out, "Alicia, it's not his fault." But he was finding it hard to talk. I asked Alicia if she could get him a coffee and plenty of sugar, which she did. Westy was able to recount the event to her.

One thing for sure—if I had lost that fight, Westy and I would have been in serious trouble, and he knew that. I never told anyone about that night and the Club were none the wiser. I didn't go out much as it was, and that night made me realise that you were far better off not doing so. The punk got everything he deserved that night, and he would never have forgotten it. I often wondered how many poor bastards had the shit kicked out of them by these cowards, and also pondered whether they had learnt a lesson that night. Who knows.

Working in the bank, I had a good mate, Peter Sands. Sandsy spoke fluent Polish as his parents were Polish. He had a girl-friend, Margaret, and we used to all get together reasonably often and always had a good time. One day we had a BBQ and a few hours later, Sandsy pulled me aside and wanted to tell me something. He went on to explain that Margaret had money missing out of her purse, which was in her bag. I asked him how much and he said $20. I felt a knot tighten in my guts and he went on to say that this was the second time it had happened, and both he and Margaret knew Alicia was the culprit.

Almost whispering, he told me what a great mother Alicia was and that she appeared to be a terrific wife but for this problem, and I should have a serious talk to her. I agreed and promised to give Margaret $20. Sandsy didn't want the $20 and instead he implored me to speak with Alicia. He told me if Alicia continued doing this, then he and Margaret could not continue to be our friends. I fully understood and promised him I would speak with Alicia that night. I never let on to Sandsy that there had been problems of this nature in the past.

That night I spoke with Alicia about my conversation with Pete, and as usual she flatly denied it. She was more upset about being accused; but I just knew she had done it, and that this wouldn't be the last time. I let Alicia know that I was starting to feel a lot of shame about all of this, and she needed to stop stealing. She didn't take it on board, and instead got into me about doubting my own wife. The situation was just bloody hopeless. The only thing keeping me in the marriage was beautiful little Tanya. I wouldn't ever abandon my little girl. Never. The marriage to Alicia was going to be a love-hate one for its entire duration.

The 1974 season came and went. I was back to playing State football and finished high up in the Fairest and Best count. Except for a few games, I was very happy with the season and the way I played. I tried wearing sports glasses and they were a dismal failure, so I went back to substandard contact lenses, which were better than nothing. The eye issue was a pain in the arse; but I also had to contend with a dislocated right shoulder which popped straight back in again, but I was really sore, and I carried it for weeks. On top of this, I received a couple of cracked ribs, but just had to get on with it. Swans had improved even more, and we won eleven games and drew one. We finally made it into the Finals.

One memorable game was against East Perth at Perth Oval. I was up against my future Fitzroy teammate, Ron Alexander. Ronny was a big boy, standing around 198cm and weighing 110kg. I was having a good day using my leap to good advantage, and to this day I have no idea why I hatched a silly plan with my ruck rover, Greg Latham. Greg was a big solid boy, approximately 185cm and 90kg or a little more. Ten minutes before half time, I told Greg that I would come in the same way as Ronny and wrestle with him at the next centre bounce, if the umpire had to conduct a second bounce.

"I want you to line Ronny up and take him out," I said.

"No worries, mate," he said.

The situation arose and I came in with Ronny, waiting in anticipation for Greggy's arrival, and arrive he did. I felt as though a tractor had just hit me and it felt as though my left knacker was in my mouth and I was about to cough it out. I was in a sorry state and went down for a few minutes. I then limped off to the forward pocket for recovery time, and was in a lot of pain. Ronny skipped down to the back pocket as happy as Larry. "Bobby, I've come down here just in case you kick some goals. I'm not allowed to let you kick goals."

"Don't worry, Ronny. The way I feel, you won't have to worry about me for a while," I grimaced.

I got into the rooms and went straight up to Greg.

"What the fuck did you do? You were supposed to hit him, not me."

"Oh, he moved, mate," he replied sheepishly.

Apparently, Ronny had pushed me into Greg's path when he saw what was coming at him. I had my eyes on the ball.

I looked at Greg and groaned. "Fuck me drunk. What a fuck up..." I said, walked off, licked my wounds, and got ready for the second half without any further plans.

Swans beat Subiaco in the first semi-final, 99 to 76. We played Perth in the Preliminary Final and went down 69 points to 84. Our woeful kicking 9 goals 15 points killed us. We should have been playing in a grand final, but that's football. A game of both mental and physical pain.

A couple of weeks after this, the players and their wives and girlfriends all got together at a teammate's house for a BBQ and a few drinks. It was a good day, and towards the end one of my mates came over and told me someone had taken money out of some of the girls' bags. The bags were all on a double bed in one of the bedrooms, and I knew Alicia had been in and out of the room getting things for Tanya. I got that same feeling in my guts again and just went along with my mate's story, saying things like, "Fuck, I wonder who would do that?"

On the way home, I told Alicia about the conversation, and she said the women were also talking about it. I looked at her and said, "I'm not accusing you, Alicia, but do you know anything about it?"

She got angry and denied having anything to do with it. Deep down, I just knew it was Alicia. But what the hell could I do? After this, I would go to the Club functions but not to BBQs or other people's places if I could possibly avoid them. This shit was really starting to get me down and I was looking forward to getting over to Victoria and starting fresh. Well, there was another shock on its way.

I had done my two years as was agreed between Stan Moses and me, with a handshake to boot. I got stuck into training at the end of October in preparation for the upcoming season, which I thought would be with Fitzroy. Early December, I spoke with Moses in his office at Bassendean Oval.

He eyed me from his side of the desk and said, "The Club is not going to clear you next season, 1975. They want one more year from you and then will work out an arrangement with Fitzroy FC."

I could not believe what I was hearing. I stared at him and told him he had gone back on his word, and I was going anyway. Moses said it was a Committee decision and if I went, the Club would make me stand out of football for a year. And he was right, that's what clubs could and would do in those days. I got up and walked out of his office, absolutely gutted. There was no way I was prepared to stand out of football for a year so here I was, completely trapped and dealing with people I could not trust.

I had a long conversation with Bruce Wilkinson, the Secretary of Fitzroy, and in the end the best thing I could do was to put in one more good year and then get into the car and drive to Melbourne without even talking to the Club. That was the plan, and come hell or high water, that was exactly what I was going to do.

I had some good mates in Greg Murray, Max George, and Gary McDonald. We would hang around on the weekends playing backyard cricket and having a few beers plus going to other places, and so on; stuff that most young people do. These times and my training helped me to get over the disappointment of Swans and how they had behaved. I became determined to have a good season in 1975 and then set about achieving that goal.

By this stage, I had left the bank and started selling life insurance for MLC, and was doing reasonably well. The money was way better than the bank had paid me. I still saw Gary Bowden, and he invited Alicia and me over to his place for a drink at his mother's house, as he was living there at the time. Gary's brother Frank was also there. Frank looked like a '60s rock star, albeit without the long hair. He was a good looking fellow with a warming personality.

The only problem with Frank was that he strayed to the shady side of the law from time to time. On this particular night, Frank explained that the heat on him in Perth was getting too much and he had to get out. Apparently, he had been involved in the Vox Adeon job. Vox Adeon was a huge electrical store in Perth during the '70s, and it was broken into and robbed by a well-organised gang. Whether Frank was truly involved or not, I didn't know.

Alicia and I were going up to the farm to visit Mum and Dad on the upcoming Friday night and I asked Frank if he was up to a bit of farm work, as Dad could arrange a job for him. Frank jumped at the chance, so I rang Dad and he told me they needed an extra bloke to work with him on the sheep. We took Frank to the farm on the Friday night, and he fitted in very well. He stayed at the bunkhouse and according to Dad, Frank was a good worker and a nice fellow to work with. Both Mum and Dad liked him. Frank worked on the farm for somewhere between six and twelve months and then disappeared back into Perth. I never saw him again.

The 1975 season was almost upon us, and I had another big preseason and was excitedly looking forward to getting stuck into it. I had a very good season, and at the end of it, Swans had won 13 games—another improvement—and headed for a second Finals series in a row. We had finished second on the ladder and readied ourselves for the second Semi-Final against West Perth, who had finished top of the ladder. By game's end Swans had been beaten 142 points to 64. It was a dismal effort and I felt we had gone into this game way too top heavy. There were too many big blokes against the speed of West Perth.

Although we lost this game, we still had another chance. We had to get ready now for the preliminary Final against South Fremantle. As I was getting out of bed on Sunday morning, I stood up and my knee locked. I couldn't bend my right leg, so I hobbled for a bit, then it released and went back to normal. The following week at training, it locked again, then released. The Club doctor told me it appeared to be a cartilage problem; and now it was giving me a bit of pain.

The day before the game, a couple of doctors injected the knee from the front into the joint. Jack was with me, and I don't know what they put into it but they said this would get me through the game, and it did. If I was in the same position today, would I have let them do it? No. The game went ahead and at the end, Swans went down to Souths 106 points to 93. We went in with a much quicker side and played all over South Fremantle, but woeful kicking for goal cost us the game. At the end of the day, we had kicked 12 goals, 21 points, a disgraceful effort.

I went straight into hospital and had my right knee operated on. The surgeon took out pieces of torn cartridge and told me it was a bit of a mess. The knee got infected, and the pain was almost unbearable. At that stage, I didn't think I would walk again, let alone play football. Eventually the knee was brought under control, and I started on rehab. By mid-December, I was back to running and the knee felt good.

In the meantime, the Swan medal for the Fairest and Best award had taken place. I had finished second, just pipped for the medal by my good mate Gary McDonald. I was very pleased for him, as he'd had a good season and deserved to win. I was also happy with my season and felt all the hard work had paid off.

Now I needed to get ready to head off to Melbourne and pit myself against the best footballers in the country. I always wanted to go as far as possible with footy. I would have found it hard to live with myself had I just stayed and played my whole career in WA, and I didn't ever want to be left wondering whether I could have made it in the VFL. It was now or never.

As December 1975 approached, Alicia and I decided to jump into the car and drive to Melbourne. Fitzroy would pay for the removalist, and we would leave around the 15th of December and get to Melbourne before Christmas. There would be no meeting with Swans as I couldn't trust them anymore, so there would be no going away party. We would just go.

A week before we left, my good mate Gary McDonald came around and wanted me to travel to Coorow with him. It was to be a road trip to say goodbye; well, a huge piss-up, to be honest. He begged Alicia to let me go and she agreed. She said she would pick me up in a couple of days.

Macca's parents had a farm at Coorow, which is a little place not far from Moora. Moora is a regional town about 180km north of Perth in the wheatbelt region of WA, with a population of between 1500 and 2000.

Macca had purchased an old Vanguard ute which he paid $35 for, and let me tell you, it looked every inch a $35 vehicle; it was a real piece of shit. But he was confident we would make it. He had a big esky on the seat which was full to the brim, and he remarked that there was a bottle of Cold Duck rosé at the very bottom and by the time we got to that we would be very wobbly. I asked Macca why we had so much water on the back, "Oh, I forgot to tell you, Schneider," (this was his nickname for me), "the ute boils over every 20-30km and we have to fill the radiator. Also, the top speed is around 30 to 35 kilometres per hour." Say what? This was getting worse by the minute.

We hit the road and got stuck into the wallop. It was going to be a long trip. As the journey wore on, we had been in and out of the ute quite often, pouring water into the radiator, and I reckon I could have run faster than the heap of shit anyway. Macca looked across at me and beamed.

"She goes all right, don't ya reckon, Schneider?"

I pissed myself laughing and commented, "No she fucking doesn't, Macca."

It was taking forever, and a few hours in we had to take on more water so we stopped off at the odd dam to fill the containers. Macca asked if I could drive for a bit, which I did. As I was taking off, I accidentally ran over a white post, which didn't seem to worry Macca at all. He had a good laugh and uttered, "Keep her on the road if you can, Schneider."

I drove for about an hour and it was very slow. So slow that Macca told me he had noticed my whiskers had grown in the time we had been on the road. The esky was emptying by this stage, and I could see the Cold Duck at the bottom. We had a helluva good time on the journey, and when we pulled into the farm at Coorow, the esky was empty. Cold Duck and all. I was totally done, as was Macca. Not far from the house, I spotted an above ground pool which had muddy dam water in it. I jumped in, clothes and all, and sat at the bottom, coming up for air and then sinking back down again. After a while I went inside, got changed and went to sleep for a fair while.

The next thing I knew, Alicia was there telling me it was time to go. We headed off on the long drive across the Nullarbor on our way to Melbourne. Tanya was just over four years old.

5
THRUST INTO
THE BIG TIME

IN THOSE DAYS, A FAIR BIT OF THE DRIVE WAS ON UNSEALED road. It was very dusty, extremely bumpy, and slow. The trip was rougher than we had expected, but we eventually made it to Melbourne and were met at Rockbank by Club Assistant Secretary Kevin Dixon, who guided us into the city, a distance of roughly 35km. We stayed in a hotel-motel for a couple of weeks until a house could be found.

Around a week after arriving in Melbourne, I came down with the mumps, a viral infection that knocked the hell out of me. After four weeks, I started to feel reasonably normal again and started my running and weights in preparation for a big preseason.

Fitzroy wanted to put me through a thorough medical examination as they had concerns about my knee and the shoulder which had been dislocated at Swans. The examination would be conducted by Club doctor and former Australian tennis player, John Fraser. He was a very likeable and affable man.

John tested everything, and lastly, he focused on my right shoulder, going through all the movements trying to get a wince or any sign of discomfort. At the end, he instructed me to give him a hard bump with the shoulder. I went at him from a metre away, and whack! The doc hit the wall with a thud and was a bit shaken up.

"Christ, not that bloody hard!" he yelled as he started rubbing his shoulder.

The Fitzroy administrators in the room could not contain their laughter, with one commenting, "Well, I think his shoulder is pretty good, Doc."

I looked over at Doc Fraser and said, "Well, you wanted me to give you a bump, Doc."

"Just not that bloody hard."

The test was over, and I passed.

By January we were well and truly into preseason, and as expected it was gruelling. The 1976 season was one I would like to forget. I could not get going and was playing in all sorts of positions and really struggling. After training one night, I approached the coach, Kevin Rose, and asked him if he could leave me in one position so I could settle down. Rose got abusive and carried on like a pork chop. He told me I'd play where he told me to play and if I didn't like it, I could leave. And he added no player had ever left him before. Max George, my teammate from Swans, walked out of Fitzroy after just five games, so he got that one wrong. I stared at Rose in disbelief and told him that his attitude was ordinary and then just walked away.

The whole season had started off badly, with Swans making it clear that I would not be cleared. The situation really stressed me out and I was filthy with the Swan Districts Football Club. This was how they were treating one of their own after six seasons of excellent service. The clearance eventually came through at 6pm on the Friday night before my first game against Richmond at the MCG. In all, I played 13 league games and 9 in the reserves.

I felt homesick, depressed and very alone. I wrote a long letter to my old coach Jack, and he wrote back telling me to stick at it and how much he believed in me. I was so grateful to get that letter from Jack. At season's end, Fitzroy had won seven games out of 22. I did a lot of soul searching at season end and realised failure was not an option. I did a huge weights program under the guidance of Maurie Raynor, an ex-surf lifesaving Iron Man champion.

The 1977 preseason was the biggest I had done. It was obvious that Kevin Rose and I didn't have a lot in common and we didn't speak to each other unless it was necessary or football business. Fitzroy were desperate for a full forward and Rose decided to put me there and leave me in that position. The success of this move was immediate, and I started to really fire. Although the Club had only won six games in 1977, I had a very good year and booted 59 goals and played 21 games.

During the season, we played a home game against Essendon at the Junction Oval. I was sitting in my car with Alicia and Tanya after the game, and just about to drive out of the car park. A fellow of about 20 years of age walked up to the car and started to swear and throw abuse at us, and then began to spit at the car. He was around 180cm tall and reasonably well built, with a good mop of hair. I noticed some heavy rings on his fingers. He walked around to my side, swearing profusely.

My window was down, and he looked as though he was about to throw a punch through the open window and into my face. I forced my door open quickly and laid into him. I grabbed a handful of hair and belted his head into the car next door several times. He was spent and in big trouble, because I would not stop once the rage was in me. All of a sudden, I was attacked from behind by three of his mates and wore a few before a couple of umpires came in to help. His mates ran off.

I got a call from the Sergeant at St Kilda Police Station on Sunday morning, and he told me that four of the attackers were in the lock-up and asked if I would press charges. He told me that the main offender had copped a lot of punishment from the fight and was feeling very sore and sorry for himself.

I said, "Well, that's good enough punishment. I won't press charges."

Weeks later, I was at the Melbourne markets with Alicia when I spotted the bloke. He was running his father's shoe shop. He came straight up to me and apologised for his behaviour and told me I was the best bloke in the world for dropping the charges. He said that his father was Greek, and would have killed him. He offered me free shoes, which I declined, and he kept shaking my hand. He told me he would never take on another footballer as he couldn't believe how strong I was. I told him everything was good and not to worry about it, shook his hand for the tenth time, and walked off. I guess he learnt a big lesson out of the incident.

During the season, I was approached by a Fitzroy supporter named Alan Greenhill. Alan was a well-known optometrist and told me he had noticed that my eyes were affecting my game and asked if I would pay him a visit in the city to have them tested, adding that he would not charge me as he loved Fitzroy and would do it for the Club. I agreed, and lost count of the trips into the city to see Alan. He was the most persistent and focused person I had met, and the word "failure" was not in his vocabulary.

Alan explained that I had very bad stigmatisms on both eyes and that the contact lenses I needed would be extremely difficult to make, but he was willing to give it a go if I was. It took disappointment after disappointment and many visits to Alan's practice over months, but eventually Alan succeeded in making lenses for my eyes. We were both over the moon, and for the first time in my career I could clearly see the ball. The experience was a new lease of life for me and gave me a huge lift. I owe so much to Alan Greenhill and he is a person that I will never forget. He's an absolute hero in my book.

My son Brett was born on the 28th of October 1977. It was a bit of a shock as Alicia had explained that she had a problem with her ovaries after Tanya was born and it would be difficult to have any more children. So here we were with a healthy bouncing boy born some six and a half years after Tanya. Alicia was in her element and made friends with the neighbours. She was enjoying her time in Melbourne.

Kevin Rose was replaced as coach by Graeme Campbell for the 1978 season. Graeme was a former Fitzroy player and had been living and coaching in Western Australia. He was easy to get on with and good to talk to. And he had a bubbly, infectious personality. I started to feel comfortable with VFL football now, and playing in a set key position was a godsend.

Weight training became a huge part of my preseasons, as I needed the extra strength to play full forward. Practising my goalkicking became second nature now, and endless hours were spent on this. My strength had increased to such an extent that I was able to bench press 300 pounds (137kg).

The VFL held a night Premiership competition called the Escort Cup and these games were played under lights at VFL park. Fitzroy made the Grand Final of this competition, and we took on the mighty North Melbourne side, who were coached by Ron Barassi and were chocbloc with stars all over the ground. We went in as absolute underdogs and ended up walloping North 13 goal 18 points (96) to 2.8 (20). It was a real highlight and the 27,000 people there went nuts, particularly our loyal, long-suffering fans. Fitzroy won nine games for the season, which was a little disappointing, but we players knew there were good days just around the corner. I had another very good season kicking 65 goals and a ten-goal haul against South Melbourne at the Junction Oval in round four. Fitzroy had fought back from a long way down to get up and win the duel in the end. It was one of the best wins I had been involved with.

During the off season of 1978, the Club received some bad news. Graeme Campbell had to return to Western Australia for family reasons. I was disappointed, as he was such a good coach to play under and had lifted the Club to a new level and was about to reap the rewards of his work. Now the Club had to find a new coach, and he came along in the form of Bill Stephen. Billy was a former Fitzroy and State player for Victoria and was extremely experienced where football was concerned. He had been an assistant to Barrassi at North Melbourne, and had coached the Essendon side. Billy developed the young players at Essendon, including Watson, Nagle, Merrett, and they became known as the Baby Bombers. Kevin Sheedy was to reap the rewards of Billy's hard work for many years to follow. Bill Stephen was one of the best people I have ever met. He was nature's gentleman and became a lifelong friend of mine until he sadly passed away on the 23rd of August 2020. Just like Graeme Campbell, Billy was very approachable and had a terrific demeanour about him.

The preseason was a typically gruelling one, but that was something I was now used to. Prior to the season proper, we played a combined New South Wales side at the Sydney Showgrounds as part of the preseason competition. NSW were coached by Alan Jeans of Hawthorn fame. I had to wear sports glasses once again in this game, as I had lost a contact lens and was waiting for a new one to be made. NSW came out firing and by half time they were in front. This was to be the one and only time I ever witnessed Billy lose his temper, and he really gave it to us at half time. Fitzroy responded to that blistering tongue lashing, and we ran out comfortable winners, 133 points to 77. I kicked six goals and it was the last time I would ever wear sports glasses.

The 1979 season was a standout for Fitzroy. We won 15 games for the year and played in two finals. The elimination final was played against Essendon, and we thrashed them. The following week, we went up against Collingwood at the MCG in front of a crowd of 90,000 people. Unfortunately, Fitzroy went down by 17 points. Both finals were sudden death as we had been beaten in our last home and away game by Geelong, thus forfeiting a double chance which ended up costing us dearly. But that's football and there is little point dwelling on it. Personally, I couldn't have been happier with my year, having played in all 22 games plus two finals, and I kicked a Club record score of 87 goals.

The one thing that eluded me during my time in Melbourne was finding a decent job, something with a future. So here I was in 1980, working as a maintenance man at the Junction Oval. It was a real dead-end position with no future. All the jobs I had while in Melbourne were just fill-in occupations such as hotel work, crap sales work, and an absolute waste of time office position—no future whatsoever. I spoke to the Club about my situation and asked if they could help secure me a position to learn groundsman skills, as I could see future benefit there. But nothing ever came of it, and I worked at the Junction Oval for a year.

We got over the disappointment of losing to Collingwood in 1979 and it was full bore into 1980. I put in three hugely solid months of preseason and then hurt my back badly in late December 1979. The injury caused me to lose coordination on my left side so that my left leg would collapse under me. I was bent over for a few weeks and the pain was terrible. I was sent to see Dr Howard Toyne.

Dr Toyne was a pioneer of sports science in Australia and worked with the 1956 and 1964 Olympic teams; he was also a surgeon. Howard had a connection with Fitzroy and after examining me he told me I had lost coordination in my left leg and then went on to explain how to get right again. He put me onto heavy-duty anti-inflammatory drugs and got me onto a stretching apparatus. The stretching was done on a flat table with ropes, weights and a wheel, to apply more and more pressure. This went on for a few weeks and then it was into the pool for more rehab, plus a lot of swimming to keep up some fitness. After a couple of months, I came good and it was back into football training.

I was a fair way behind now as I had lost a couple of months of the hard grind of a preseason schedule. I will always be grateful to Howard Toyne for his assistance in getting me over the back injury and back into footy again. Where 1979 had been so excitingly successful for Fitzroy, the 1980 season was the polar opposite. We won only four games for the season and lost a few close ones, but just could not get going. I couldn't understand how we had gone from such a gun side to a very ordinary side in such a short time, but there it was.

My season was reasonable. I ended up kicking 63 goals but, like everyone else, I was very disappointed with the whole affair. While the job at the Junction Oval was a dead end one, I at least had plenty of laughs during its duration. I found myself working with two teammates, Leigh McConnon and Brett Grimley. I was put in charge of these two, as the Club put it, so that we could get some work out of them. Good luck with that one!

Leigh was a gentleman, very considerate with good manners. He was 177cm tall but was very quick and had won a few professional foot races in Tasmania before joining Carlton, where he played approximately 30 games. He came across to Fitzroy in 1980. Leigh reminded me of Clark Gable, the actor, so I referred to him as Miniature Clark. Brett Grimely was nineteen and 190cm tall, and came to Fitzroy from Queensland. Grimma was confident, maybe a little too confident at times, and loved to play pranks whenever the opportunity arose. He also had a very inquisitive nature and was prone to a bit of homesickness. Alicia looked after him like a mother whenever he visited our home.

The Club wanted the three of us to paint the grandstand seats a few days prior to a home game. They were to be painted white. I got the boys organised and we started the job. Paint was being slapped around like there was no tomorrow, then all hell broke loose. Grimma accused Leigh of flicking some paint on him and slapped the brush full of paint across Leigh's face. Leigh chased Grimma up and down the grandstand, hell bent on restitution.

In the end, I got hold of Grimma and kept Leigh off him and brought some calm to the situation. We all got on and finished the job. Saturday arrived and the stands were full. After the game, a few of the women were not happy. Apparently, glob-ules of paint had formed under the seats along the front edges and were like bubbles waiting to burst; and the women had put their hands on their lovely outfits only to see white paint all over their slacks and dresses. This only occurred in one reasonably small section of the seats, but it was enough to cause quite the stir.

Another job I did was to rake the clay tennis courts by drag-ging a contraption behind the tractor. The courts had a three-metre concrete wall on one side, which had a gate in the middle. While driving around, I noticed Grimma and Leigh with an extension ladder and a couple of 20-litre containers. They walked across the court and through the gate. I asked myself what the hell they would be doing, but then just forgot about it and continued on. I was doing a final run alongside the big wall when all of a sudden, I was hit with a torrent of water. I jumped about a foot off the seat and couldn't work out what the hell was going on. It gave me a real start. I looked up and saw them on top of the wall, laughing hysterically. Well, it was either kill the pair of them or just laugh with them. I chose the latter and became a lot more vigilant where those two buggers were concerned.

Grimma would refer to Leigh as the little man, which to Leigh was just water off a duck's back. He was very laid back; and not too much bothered Miniature Clark at all, except when Grimma just got a little too much, which was reason-ably often. Leigh would come up to me with a concerned look at times and in a whisper would ask, "Hey, Clark, where's that fucking prick? I need to go and have a crap and I don't want him knowing which toilet I'm in. I will go over to the toilets on the far side of the ground. Mate, for Christ's sake, don't let him know where I am." Leigh referred to me as Clark because he thought I looked like Clark Kent. Grimma had nailed poor Leigh twice with 20 litres of water over the dunny door and he would come out looking as though he had been presoaked in a washing machine. The little man was now getting paranoid about Grimma's movements when it came to toilet time.

We used to eat lunch in the cricketers' viewing room at the Junction Oval. Leigh purchased a carton of eggnog and left it in the sun for a few days, opening it slightly so it wouldn't explode. He brought it over to me when Grimma wasn't around and in a very quiet tone explained, "Clark, I'm going to put this on the floor in the lunchroom. It's bloody ripe, mate, been in the sun for three days. You know what Grimma is like, mate, he can't walk past anything without poking it, kicking it or stomping on it. I bet you he will try and flatten this eggnog. Now keep an eye on him, Clark, and make sure you are not near the bloody thing."

"No worries, mate. I'll sit well away. Let's see what happens."

We drove the small Jeep down to our favourite lunch bar in Chappell Street and all of a sudden Grimma was crouched right down so that it looked as though it was only Leigh and I in the vehicle. We looked like two male lovers driving down the street. Leigh was beside himself and yelling at Grimma, and trying to pull him up at the same time.

"Get up, you fucking moron, Grimma. What are all these people going to think? They will think Clark and I are gay! Get up, you idiot!"

Grimma stayed there until we were parked, and we all got out. I started to piss myself laughing. Not so much at Grimma, who was hysterical by now, but more at the look of disgust on Leigh's face. He was like a dad telling his son off for being naughty. We got back to the Junction Oval and started lunch. Grimma walked past the eggnog carton and sat down. He looked at the carton a few times, Leigh and I watching like hawks. We finished lunch and Grimma made a beeline for the carton, which he assumed was empty, and at the same time Leigh and I headed hastily for the open door. As we got to the door, we both turned at the same time and there he was, about two feet airborne directly above the putrid eggnog. Down he came with a wallop, a direct hit. The eggnog burst out of the carton and went everywhere. The smell was horrific and there was Grimma standing there with the shit all over him and everywhere else. He looked like a stunned mullet and knew he had made an enormous error of judgement assuming the carton was empty. Grimma had to shower and then clean up the mess. As for Leigh and me, we could not stop laughing. After it was all over, Grimma kept saying, "Who would leave a full milk carton on the floor like that? I thought it was empty. Fucking idiots." Leigh and I got a lot of mileage out of that day.

As well as the maintenance work at the ground, the three of us were also responsible for setting up functions held under the Blackie Ironmonger Grandstand, and then dismantling and putting away all the settings as well as cleaning the place in readiness for the next one. A huge group of well-known Aussie actors would get together now and again for a long, long lunch, and one of those was held at the Junction Oval in the Fitzroy Sports and Social Club, which was situated at the city end of the ground. I had worked at the Union Hotel, on the corner of Union Street and Chapel Street, for a year after first arriving in Melbourne in 1976. The Club asked me if I would work behind the bar for this particular function and I readily agreed.

This was a big gathering, and the boys were keen to get into a few drinks right away. Action behind the bar was frantic as they all piled up and I was blown away, even a little starstruck, as I had only seen these guys on TV shows such as Homicide, Division 4, The Box, Number 96, Solo One, Bluey and a host of other shows. Here I was serving them grog. Maurie Fields was a standout with his unique voice and humour; then there were George Mallaby, Alwyn Kurts, Norman Yem, Gerard Kennedy, and the list went on and on. It was a very busy day, and I enjoyed every minute of my time. There was not one of these people that had an opinion of themselves. They were all humble, well-mannered individuals who knew how to have a good time.

After one particular large function under the Blackie Ironmonger stand, the boys and I had to dismantle the setting and clean the place up. It was a Monday morning, and the lads were a little sluggish. Without any lights on, the room was pitch black; you couldn't see your own finger 10cm in front of your face, it was so dark down there. On this occasion, Grimma came up with another plan to put some fun into the task. Two of us would hide in the dark and the other would have to come into the room, navigate through the darkness and try to find one of the two. We would then rotate so that each of us had a turn at finding someone in the dark. The two inside would have five minutes to ready themselves. We would set up obstacles such as tables, chairs, and brooms placed across chairs, so that the person entering would crash into them and we would know roughly where they were.

When it came to Grimma's turn to be the one on his own, he refused to comply; you could see he was fearful of the dark, and of course he didn't trust Leigh and me one bit. We appealed to his manliness and cajoled him for about ten minutes. At last, Grimma reluctantly agreed to take his turn, but it had been hard work to convince the bugger to take his rightful turn. Grimma went outside and Leigh and I went to work. We set up all of the obstacles and then I gave Leigh a big bunch of balloons and a pen to burst them at the right time. Leigh stood at the last obstacle with his balloons, and I stood near the light switches. Grimma entered and we could tell he was nervous as a kitten just by his voice.

"Where are you, little man? I know I'm near you, little man." Then CRASH, as he went over the first obstacle and hit the floor. "Fuck, I'm going to kill you, little man, when I find you." Then another crash and more expletives.

One more crash bang to go and he would be, unbeknown to him, right near the little man. The final obstacle went down, and Leigh popped the balloons in quick succession, making a hell of a racket. I flicked on the lights and there was Grimma, lying on the floor in fetal position, numb with terror.

Leigh and I doubled over laughing and Leigh managed to blurt out, "You're terrified of the dark, you big girl!"

Grimma sprang up and lunged at Leigh. They both hit the floor and once again were into it. I rushed over and separated them, then started laughing again. Then we all laughed and carried on. We got back to work and finished the job. Whilst we made our own fun, the work always got done. I will never forget working with those two boys and the amount of fun we had.

Fitzroy were struggling financially by 1980 and I was tired of asking for my money all the time. Sometimes I would have to ask three or four times, and I found it embarrassing and stressful. The other thing that concerned me was the question of worthwhile employment and my future. This was weighing on my mind heavily, and in around November I decided to leave Fitzroy and play with Woodville in Adelaide. Had I been employed in a decent job, I would never have left Fitzroy at the end of 1980.

PHOTO GALLERY

My great friends Leigh
Andrewartha (Dommy) and
his wife Julie. We had many
wonderful times together.

Michael and Tanya at their wedding reception. My mate Dommy is in the background.

My business partner Ash Floyd
(Ash the Flash) we were like
brothers sadly he passed away
in 2001 aged just 51 years.

Ingrid, Mum, Dad and Me all
dressed up as neat as a pin.

My mother with Ingrid and Me.

Ingrid, Dad, Mum and Me.

My grandfather and
grandmother with my
dad Jimmy as a baby.
Dad was born in 1911.

My mother not long after
arriving in Australia.

Mum holding Jane Fowler when working for the Tommy Fowler Family.

Mum with Harry Hanson.
Harry was a true gentleman
and valued family friend.

Tanya nursing her brother Brett.
This was in my football memorabillia
as Alicia never left me a single family
photo.

This photo was also in my
football memorabillia. Tanya
and our beautiful dog Sabby
in the early seventies.

After 50 years I finally caught up
with my mate 'Shorty'.

My good friend Alan Swain, 'Swainy',
from Encounter Bay F.C.

From Left, my brother-in-law
Bazza, Ingrid and Aaron.

Aaron and Mum in Narrogin.

Mum and Dad
in their later years.

In Thailand at age 57.
I had just scaled approx.
1,400 steps to get to the
Big Buddha Statue. Quite
taxing getting to the top.

Bazza and Dad in Narrogin.

Bazza, Dad and Me in Narrogin.

Jimmy in the kitchen in Narrogin. He was in his early nineties.

From left, Aunty Ella (Dad's sister),
Dad and Mum in Narrogin.

Mystique Cottage.
Northam looking from
Goomalling Road.

The patio at Mystique Cottage.
Where Shelley and I spent a
lot of time.

My beautiful little dog Millie.

Millie's Cottage.
Mount Barker, WA
Circa 1920, now restored.

Duke St Northam.
Restored to a
beautiful property.

My first job in Melbourne, working at the Union Hotel, 1976.

At the Hall of Fame
Night with my mate
Charlie Burnett.

Inducted into the
Encounter Bay F.C.
Team Of The Century.

TEAM OF THE CENTURY

1921   2021

ENCOUNTER BAY
Football Club

1st. RUCK
Andrew McLean
Tyson Davis-Neale
Marty Fraser

2nd. RUCK
Robert Beecroft
Noel Clark
David Pearson

Coach
Doug Tugwell

Captain
Don Bartel

Robert Beecroft
FORWARD POCKET

Tony Modra
FULL FORWARD

David Pearson
FORWARD POCKET

James West
HALF FORWARD FLANK

Allan Field
CENTRE HALF FORWARD

Peter Johnston
HALF FORWARD FLANK

Don Bartel
WING

Lyndon Elsworthy
CENTRE

Peter Millard
WING

David Shegog
HALF BACK FLANK

Frank Joy
CENTRE HALF BACK

Reg Masters
HALF BACK FLANK

Trevor Prior
BACK POCKET

Ian Millard
FULLBACK

Rigby Barnes
BACK POCKET

Interchange
Jack Roads (Senior)
Steven Hann
Craig Littlely
Bert Hutton
Greg Brand
Noel Clark
Tony Proud

Vice Captain
Peter Millard

Deputy Vice Captain
Tyson Davis-Neale

Presented to:- 　　　　　 **25th April 2021**

Bill Stephen, a great coach
and a magnificent man.
We became close friends.

* Page 2 — The Sun, Monday, July 30, 1979

● FITZROY coach Bill Stephen.

A Footy Card—1970.
My first year in League Football.

Leigh McConnon (Miniature Clark)
just before he came to Fitzroy.
A fine human being.

Meeting Prince Charles
at the Oval prior to an
Exhibition Game in 1972.
He is being introduced by
Carlton great John Nicholls.
Prince Phillip was also
introduced to the players.

A 22 year drought
finally broken.
Premiers 1989.
Encounter Bay
Football Club.

ENCOUNTER BAY FOOTBALL CLUB
A GRADE PREMIERS G.S.F.L. 1989

BACK ROW: G. ROBERTS (SECRETARY), A. HORROCKS, A. PEARSON, L. ELLSWORTHY,
A. GUY, J. GUY, G. BRAND, A. COUZNER, D. RADY, P. TONKIN (RUNNER)
MIDDLE ROW: G. STOCK (PRESIDENT), R. SMITH (TRAINER), K. RUSSELL, A. DAVIS,
S. CRANE, D. GUEST, T. ALMOND, J. AINSWORTH, W. TONKIN, J. GUY (MANAGER),
A. CRISPIN (TRAINER)
FRONT ROW: W. PLUMMER (TREASURER), M. KLUSKE, B. LITTLE, K. RUGE (VICE-CAPT.),
R. BEECROFT (CAPT.-COACH), D. BROADBENT, D. PEARSON, A. CHIGWIDDEN

A boundary throw in.

A centre bounce
at Bassendean
against Claremont.

I warned Tom Grljusich
to lay off my mate Max
George. Tom took no notice
so I ironed him out but had
to go over the top of the
pack to get to him. He took
no further part in the game.

Rucking against my old foe
Mike Fitzpatrick in a final at
Subiaco in 1974. Mike was
a Rhodes Scholar as well as
a top footballer and a bloody
good bloke.

We had just beaten Barassi's North
Melbourne at Arden St in 1979.
Pictured with me is my teammate
David McMahon, pound for pound one
of the toughest players in the VFL.

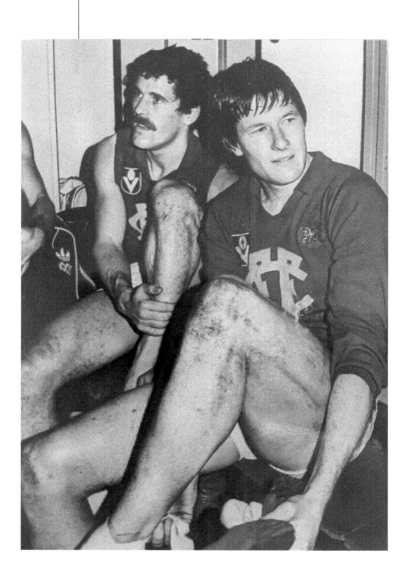

Playing in the VFL.

Taking a grab at Bassendean
against Perth F.C.

6

THE ADELAIDE YEARS

ALICIA AND I MOVED TO ADELAIDE IN LATE DECEMBER 1980 and rented a house in Netley, a suburb near Adelaide Airport. Woodville organised a job for me with Marlborough Fundraising Supplies. They supplied bingo and beer tickets and ticket-vending machines to the hotels and sporting clubs throughout South Australia. It was here I met Ash Floyd, also a West Australian and a gun salesman. Ash had charisma by the bucketful and had a one-liner or joke for every situation. He would brighten up any occasion with his quick wit and sense of humour. Ash was a couple of years older than me, and he carried a little weight and smoked like a chimney, but he didn't drink a lot. I liked Ash the minute I met him, and we were to become good mates and eventually business partners.

Woodville were a good club but always finished near the bottom of the ladder. It was going to be a hard slog, but I was up for the challenge. Ex Geelong coach Rod Olsen was appointed as coach for three years, 1981-1983. Rod was meticulous and worked really hard to get the club going. Unfortunately, he just didn't have the players. On top of that, some players just could not cope with what was required to become a good side, and were putting the knife into Rod's back, a trait shown by the weak.

We won three games in 1981, a very disappointing effort. There were just not enough good players and it was no fault of Rod Olsen, who tried everything to improve the Club. 1982 was even worse, the Club only winning one game for the year. I could see Rod was on the right track and felt we were improving. The situation reminded me of Swans when I started my career. I had been through this before and could see light at the end of the tunnel; but a lot of Woodville players had never experienced success, so all they could see was doom and gloom.

During 1982, a group of players wanted to get rid of Rod Olsen. Club Chairman, Kevin Angel, addressed the playing group. Rod Olsen was not at this meeting and after Kevin had finished, he wanted to hear from the players. A few got up and had their say. Most of it was just garbage and basically putting all the blame on poor old Rod. A senior player then got up and demanded Olsen be sacked and he said, "We would like Bob Beecroft to coach us." I was horrified to hear this and immediately got up and told Kevin Angel that I wanted no part in this at all and I was not interested in coaching the Club.

In 1982, Alicia and I had purchased some land at Hallett Cove. Hallett Cove lies 21km south of Adelaide CBD and is a coastal suburb. The land was two kilometres from the ocean and roughly three to four hundred metres from the shopping centre and tavern. The views to the ocean were magnificent. We built a house there towards the end of 1982.

During this year, Ash and I decided to start up our own fundraising business, and we called it Adelaide Fundraising

Supplies. The business took off and we were making seriously good money. Ash, myself, Alicia and Ash's wife Liz, all went to the Snooty Fox restaurant in North Adelaide to celebrate how well the business was going. On the way to the restaurant, a song came on the radio called Almost Persuaded. The song was about a fellow falling for another woman even though he was married. As things heated up, he caught the reflection of his wedding ring in this woman's eyes and didn't go through with the affair.

I told Alicia that I loved the song and she got very angry. She was angry all night and it put a damper on what should have been a celebration. Alicia would get insanely jealous where other females were concerned and was always accusing me of having affairs. There was never any problem if the female was ugly or grossly overweight. It was hard to have friends, especially if the female was half attractive, and I would find that we weren't friends for too long in cases where this applied. She would make up stories which were very uncomplimentary towards me, and tell me that's what these women were saying. I would believe her and get really pissed off and wouldn't have anything to do with the couple again. To this day I still don't know why I believed these bullshit lies. If Alicia didn't approve of a friend, she would find a way to destroy the friendship.

Anger at living like this started to build up in me. I remember visiting Mum and Dad in Narrogin, having driven over from Adelaide. Mum pulled me aside and said, "Son, why you not tell me Alicia hab cancer?" I looked at her in amazement and told her Alicia had never ever mentioned this to me. It turned out that Alicia had made up this cock and bull story as well, and I was livid with her. Did she show any remorse? None whatsoever. I wondered who else she had misled in Adelaide, and what other surprises lay in store.

Rod Olsen had one more year to run on his contract in 1983, but unfortunately Woodville decided to get rid of him. They appointed Malcolm Blight to coach instead. Rod wanted to see out his contract and while Malcolm played there as Captain; then Rod would bow out and Malcolm would take over as coach. I felt this was the way to go but Malcolm would have none of it. All Rod needed was a few more decent players. A coach is only as good as his players, as Malcolm would find out.

Another grueling preseason was done and we were into the new season of 1983. Woodville won four games and finished 10th on the ladder but showed a lot of improvement. A few more good players were recruited, and this made a huge difference. I had played the year in the ruck and rested in the forward pocket, and I was happy with my form. I could see the Club going places in the next two to three years.

Hallett Cove was a great place to live, and the business was going very well. On 19th October 1983, a new member of the family arrived. My son Aaron was born six years after Brett, and well after Alicia had informed me that she was not able to have any more children. She had led me to believe that due to a problem with her ovaries, it would be impossible to have any more children. I didn't want any more children anyway, so it was all fine by me. Aaron was a beautiful, strong healthy boy, and according to Alicia, a miracle baby.

Every 10 weeks, Ash and I would do a run from Adelaide up to Port Lincoln and all the places in between. The run would take four days. We would phone all the accounts, get the orders then load up and head off, towing a 7x5-foot tandem trailer which was fully loaded, and the boot of the vehicle was chockabloc as well. Ash would buy two cartons of Marlborough cigarettes and off we went. We would off-load tickets and call at every club and pub trying to get new business, and finish by about five or six pm each day. We would have a few drinks, eat, then more drinks and retire, ready to repeat the process the next day. We covered a lot of ground, including places like Port Pirie, Quorn, Port Augusta, Roxby Downs, The Yorke Peninsula, The Copper Triangle of Kadina, Moonta and Wallaroo, and many others.

We had another two-day run which encompassed the Clare Valley, Barossa, Peterborough, etc. This run was done each six weeks. After four days on the road, staying at Port Augusta and Port Lincoln, Ash and I would return to Adelaide with a sugar bag stuffed with cheques and cash. We had a safety deposit box at the Commonwealth Bank in King William Street, and after these trips we'd put a couple of grand or more into it. After a couple of years, we had a fair amount of cash there. Whilst I'd always had dead end no-future jobs, this venture was a blessing. Ash and I had complete freedom and plenty of money with no one telling us what to do. It was heaven. We drove brand new vehicles and updated them every two years.

Ash would have to buy a couple of packets of cigarettes on the way home from the four-day run to get him through, even though he had started off with two full cartons. He was like a Puffing Billy; I'd never seen anyone smoke like that before. All his vehicles had to have a windshield on the driver's side so that he could smoke while driving; this way no smoke would get into the car.

Ash had a hard life growing up. He had an alcoholic father and his mum left when he was quite young. His father was a shearer and Ash had gone to just about every school there was.

Sometimes he would be at a new school for just a week and then onto the next one. Ash loved his dad, but it was a tough life for a young fella. The fact his schooling had been so disruptive meant that Ash could not spell, so writing was extremely difficult for him; but he could read well enough to get by.

I first noticed his difficulty when he addressed cartons which had to be freighted into the country areas such as Port Pirie; you could barely make out the name as it was a sort of disguised form where the spelling wasn't right, but you saw something resembling Port Pirie.

One day I looked at a carton and said, "Ash, what the fuck is this?"

He then confided to me that he couldn't write too well as he didn't know how to spell. I felt awful after what I had said.

"Listen, mate, don't you worry about a thing. I'm going to teach you how to spell. I'm sorry I got into you; I didn't realise."

Ash's face lit up as he had been hiding this all his life. He was so glad that he had finally told me. At every opportunity that followed, I would refer to a word, any word, and get Ash to sound it out and break the word down. We went through the vowels and then I got Ash to write down the words that I gave him. He was a very quick learner and surprised me at how quickly he was able to grasp the concept of writing. I was so thrilled to be able to help my mate and he was equally thrilled with now being able to write most words.

Ash had a wicked sense of humour and he had a one-liner for everything. If someone was going to great lengths to convince us that he would be the first one to help, Ash would say, "That's not what I've heard." Or if the fellow confessed to liking a few drinks or whatever it would be: "Yeah, I've heard that." One day we stopped at a cross walk and a pregnant lady walked across. Ash looked at me with a cheeky grin, had a puff of his smoke, and muttered, "Well, that gets one question out of the road then." He had a remarkable memory for jokes and always had a good one up his sleeve. We were as close as brothers and Ash referred to me as the brother he never had. We were a tight and very good team.

On one of our trips through Peterborough, I first met Leigh Andrewartha. Peterborough is a town of approximately 1400 people and is situated 250km north of Adelaide. There were four hotels, and Leigh and his wife Julie ran and owned the Peterborough Hotel. Leigh was roughly 188cm tall and was solidly built with a handsome face and hair that resembled that of Jesus. He also had a terrific personality. His wife Julie was very attractive and hard-working, with a friendly demeanour. They made a lovely couple indeed. We hit it off straight away. Julie and Leigh were to become lifelong friends.

Preseason came around quickly for the 1984 campaign and as usual, I had started around the second week of October and was in good nick for our fitness test around mid to late December. The test consisted of a six- to eight-kilometre run, timed, and then ten 150-metre runs with jog recovery, followed by ten 100-metre sprints with jog recovery and all timed. I got through comfortably and was pretty happy with my fitness level, knowing that come early January the training would be tough—in fact, quite gruelling as usual.

I was summoned to a meeting at the Club sometime in January and as I drove to the club from Hallett Cove, I wondered what it was going to be about. The meeting was held on a Saturday afternoon. I walked into the room and seated there were Malcom Blight, his assistant John Read, and the General Manager, Geoff Hosking (a qualified accountant). Hosking was a good administrator, a figures man with little under-standing of the game of football. I took a seat and Malcolm did the talking.

He told me that the Club were paying way too much money for my services and in his opinion the original contract should never have been so "lucrative". My contract was a three-year deal worth $20,000 per season, hardly "lucrative", as he put it. In fact, they got me cheaply considering my record. Malcolm then went on to say the Club couldn't afford to pay me any more than $12,000 per season. Here I was, 32 years old and coming towards the end of my league career. They had me over a barrel and Blight knew it. I didn't show any emotion but I was seething underneath, and I just looked him in the eye and told him there was little I could do about it as my time in the game was drawing to a close and no other Club would take on a 32-year-old. I got up and left the meeting, then proceeded to drive home.

There was Malcolm Blight, slashing my contract and God knows who else's just so there was enough money to fill his own pockets. I would love to have seen his contract. The other thing that galled me with this situation was that Blight had no right whatsoever to view my contract with the Woodville Football Club or to negotiate a contract with me. He was a coach and that was it. I decided to play for two more years, as recognition was helping with the business and made it a lot easier to break the ice when trying to win new customers. I was making really good money with Adelaide Fundraising Supplies, so the money from football had become irrelevant. But the way Blight had gone about my contract business left a sour taste and I viewed him in a very different way from then onwards.

During the period of 1984 to 1986, something happened which made me feel ashamed, not while it was occurring, but after the event. On one of our trips to Port Lincoln, I met a woman named Jean. Jean was 38 years old, beautifully spoken, a little on the plump side, with dark hair, and very attractive, I was smitten by her right from the start. She worked at the hotel and had another job selling bridal wear. After a couple of trips, one thing led to another, and I embarked on a two-year affair with Jean. I saw her five times a year for two nights per trip, staying at her place.

We both developed strong feelings for each other, and Jean intimated that she wanted to spend the rest of her life with me. She would describe the sort of house we would live in and then let out a long sigh and say, "I know you will go back to your bloody wife who doesn't deserve you and your children, I just know you will." I would agree and tell her it was the kids I couldn't walk out on. It killed me to think about that, but I would have had no problem with leaving Alicia. My feelings for Jean were getting stronger and I started to realise the hurt I was causing her and the toll it was taking on me mentally. I ended the affair.

She was devastated and I felt heartbroken and ashamed of myself. I confessed the affair to Alicia and for obvious reasons the discussion didn't go well. Had it been a one-night stand, just sex, it still wouldn't be okay; but the affair with Jean had strong feelings involved. Not only had I hurt Jean, but I also hurt Alicia badly. No one deserves what I put these two women through. Out of both my marriages, Alicia is the only one that I ever cheated on. I learned my lesson well and truly about the pain such infidelity causes all parties concerned and would never repeat it again. As far as my marriage to Alicia went, well, that was doomed from the start. This had been another stupid, dumb action on my part.

The 1984 season came and went. Woodville won four games, but the improvement was noticeable. We lost a few close games and were no longer the easy beats. In fact, we were a threat to any side that played us. We were now beginning to get respect from the opposition. I went back to my usual position at full forward and booted 70 goals, playing the odd game in other positions. The 70 goals I kicked in 1984 came from only 14 games, as injury once again reared its ugly head and ruled me out for the rest of the season. I had been well on the way to booting 100 goals for the season, but that's football. It is such a cruel game at times both mentally and physically.

Malcolm played in the forward pocket alongside me and the combination worked very well. Malcolm Blight is the best footballer I ever played with; in fact, he's the best I have ever seen play the game, and I have seen a fair whack of footballers during my time. I have never witnessed anyone as good. He was beautifully balanced, strong in the hips with the ability to kick equally well with either foot, and could also take high marks; there was nothing he couldn't do on a football field.

But Malcolm had one bad habit that cost him a fair amount of pain in a game against Port Adelaide (Magpies) at Adelaide Oval. On many occasions I would lead out of the goal square at full pace and almost have the ball in my hands, when all of a sudden Malcolm would cut right across in front of me and try to mark or knock the ball out in front of him. I would have to take evasive action at the last second or so, just to avoid cleaning him up. On this particular occasion, I was on a full-blooded lead and had the ball firmly in my sight.

Going at full pelt, I spotted Malcolm coming across from my left, and I decided not to take evasive action this time. Instead, I was going to clean him up as it was far safer for me when travelling at that speed. I turned my body left and braced for the impact, the same as you would if delivering a shirtfront or shitmixer right up the middle. I hit Malcolm with huge ferocity and the next thing he was on the ground screaming in agony, rolling around immersed in a world of pain. I grabbed him to stop the rolling and told him to try and stay still. The trainers arrived and got him off the ground. The incident occurred leading towards half time.

When I got into the rooms, Malcolm was obviously in a lot of pain as he could only whisper and had apparently coughed up a bit of blood. He swallowed a handful of painkiller tablets, possibly Veganin, and eventually made his way over to me. He was hard to understand or hear at this stage, but I got the drift of the conversation.

"Look, Tim Evans has kicked seven goals so far and if we can stop him then we will win this game. You are the only one who can match his strength, so I want you to go fullback."

I went to fullback and played really well, at the same time keeping Evans goalless in the second half. Port was a gun side, and we went on to win that game.

Whilst Blight was a playing coach, he rarely trained with us. I found that baffling, as a playing coach needs to be doing the hard yakka shoulder to shoulder with his players. There were times where Blight would flog the guts out of the players and stand in the middle of the ground watching the pain. These floggings were not hard training sessions; they were worth less and totally unnecessary, and the fact he never partici-pated in any of this made it even more intolerable. I was 32 and had played a lot of footy and didn't need this crap. There were times I was still sore on a Saturday from these stupid floggings. Malcolm would join into the odd skill-based training but never did very much of the hard stuff, so I guess he must have trained away from the club. In any case, he was always fresh come Saturday. It would have been interesting to see how fresh he would have been had he endured the floggings we got on the track, particularly the older players.

The other reason I was losing respect for Blight was the way he liked to rip into individuals, tear them apart in front of their teammates. This tactic served no purpose as the player derived no benefit at all. In fact, it would make the individual feel worthless and depressed. The team should have been blasted as a whole; and if need be, individuals should be addressed behind closed doors, particularly if the conversation was not going to be pretty. That way it's between coach and player.

One of these occasions had to do with a young player, Roger Clift. Clifty made his league debut with Woodville in 1983 and was a big strong lad with a better than average leap. He showed enormous potential and as a footballer had everything going for him. With the right development and encouragement, this kid was going to be a beauty. We had a player meeting in the changerooms prior to going out onto the ground for training. Blight was going through a few things, then for no reason ripped into Clifty in a most humiliating and unnecessary manner. In the end he was screaming at Clifty. I could see the tears welling up in Roger's eyes and I recall being so pissed off with Blight.

The meeting finished and I went straight up to Clifty and put my arm around him. I could see he was extremely upset.

He needed support after this inane attack. I told him not to listen to one word that bloke had said.

"Mate, you have the football world at your feet and more ability than 95% of any player here; just believe in yourself."

Roger appeared to lose heart after this, and he ended up at North Adelaide sometime later. His father spoke to me about the incident; he was very angry. I have no idea whether he fronted Blight or not. All I know is that I witnessed a very good young player get totally and unnecessarily humiliated that day. Humiliating a player in front of his teammates in such a shameful way then expecting him to perform for you is flawed thinking. It has nothing to do with building strong character in anyone. I often wondered where Blight picked this crap up from. Victoria, no doubt.

I was seriously considering retiring from league football at the end of 1984, and it was a chance meeting I had with Jim Deane in the toilet at a pub in Adelaide that changed my mind. Jim was a legend in South Australian football, having played with Richmond in the VFL, and the South Adelaide Football Club with whom he won two Magarey Medals. The Magarey is a medal awarded for the Best Player in the league. Jimmy was a top bloke and I told him that I was retiring. He told me to play again as my form was good. He said that you are a long time retired once you finish. We also spoke about other things concerning football. After speaking with Jimmy, I decided to go one more year. During this stage of my life, years were measured by football seasons, gruelling preseasons, and then playing the games year in and year out. I didn't discuss with anyone that 1985 was going to be my last in league football.

Life at Hallett Cove was good, and the kids were happy. Tanya was now 14, Brett 8, and Aaron 2 years old. Going into

1985, I had one more monster preseason to complete and that would be it. I had suffered a fair few injuries in my 15 years of league football and also had a few operations, but it didn't worry me as I was feeling as good as ever and keen to go out on top, not limp to the line in my final year of league football. The 1985 preseason was hard but good. I was in tip top shape to go one last round at this level and really looking forward to it. Woodville won six games in 1985 but there were no thrashings like the bad old days, and we were right in most of the games that we lost. I had a strong feeling that success was just around the corner, but they would have to do it without me.

Both Malcolm Blight and I played our last game of league football against North Adelaide at Prospect Oval in the last round. Malcolm had the fanfare and a good send-off and I kept my last game to myself. Only I knew it was also my last. In fact, I should not have even played in this game, as I had torn a quad muscle in my right leg at training on the previous Tuesday. John Reid approached me on the Thursday as I had withdrawn from the side. Reidy had his reserves side in the finals and wouldn't have anyone replace me, so he virtually begged me to play on one leg. I reluctantly agreed because I had a lot of time for Reidy, so I got injected before the game. My leg felt like a lump of wood from the knee up and the painkiller crept down below my knee. What a way to finish my career. I managed to kick three goals, and after the game walked up to Malcolm and told him I'd just played my last game.

He was taken aback and said, "Bullshit, no way."

To which I replied, "Yes mate, I have had enough. I'm finished."

Malcolm phoned me prior to the 1986 season wanting me to return as there was a spot for me in the side. I thanked him for the call and said no.

One unfortunate but memorable incident, involving Robert Muir, occurred during my last season at Thebarton Oval against West Torrens. Robbie had just joined Woodville and had played for St Kilda in the VFL, which is where I first bumped into him. He was a hugely talented player who was much maligned during his playing career with St Kilda. I took an instant shine to Robbie and got on well with him; to me he was a top bloke. Robbie was 30 years old when Woodville signed him onto play. West Torrens had former Woodville and South Melbourne full forward John Roberts playing for them, and Blight instructed Robbie to play full back on Roberts, and to make Roberts' afternoon uncomfortable – meaning, make him earn any kicks he got and play very tight on him.

Robbie carried out his instructions and kept Roberts very quiet. Unfortunately, a few yobbos full of piss got stuck into Robbie in a most despicable fashion and hurled disgraceful and offensive abuse at him constantly. They were positioned behind the goals and would change ends to follow Robbie and continue on with their filth. I remember taking the last mark of the game and lining up for goal number seven or eight, and needing to use a torpedo punt to get the distance. The kick hit the boot perfectly and sailed through for a goal, and then all hell broke loose.

A trainer, Porky Crichton, ran up to me and blurted out, "Bobby! Quick, mate! Robbie Muir has jumped the fence and belted a couple of spectators, and they will kill him! Quick, mate!"

I sprinted down to the other end of the ground and there was a large group of irate spectators around Robbie. I forced my way in and saw two policemen and a couple of our trainers trying to protect him. We formed a tight ring around him and pushed towards the rooms. Some spectators were trying to punch Robbie, with others spitting and abusing him; it was a very bad position to be in. I wore a few hits, and I guess the others did also. It was absolute mayhem. Eventually we were able to get to the safety of the rooms, and I will never forget the scene in there. The only other player that went to Robbie's aid that day was Ralph Sewer, or Zip Zap, as he was known. He was a tough and talented pocket rocket with a heap of guts.

Ralphie, myself and Robbie all walked into the rooms together. There sitting on the benches were all my teammates, like little schoolboys waiting for the headmaster to address them. I couldn't believe what I was looking at. There were also a lot of hangers-on plus committee members in the room.

I lost my temper completely and verbally laid into the lot of them. "You fucking weak pack of bastards. Your team-mate could have been killed out there and here you all are. You couldn't give a fuck. No wonder you are on the bottom of the ladder. I am ashamed to call you my teammates. Fuck the lot of you."

There was stunned silence until Blight decided to have a crack at Robbie, which was super bad timing as Robbie had endured enough crap for one day. Robbie screamed something at Malcolm and then it was all over. What a clusterfuck this day had turned out to be. After the chaos I went home and reflected on the events which had unfolded, and I knew the decision I had made to retire at season's end was the right one. I had a good year in 1985 and I went out of league football contented. I had given it everything and achieved a lot out of the game. My time had come, and it was over.

For the first time in seventeen years, I gave my body a good rest. The quad muscle took six weeks to get right, and my back took around ten weeks to feel strong and normal again. I started light running with a lot of stretching and lighter weight training, and I purchased an inversion stretching machine for my back, which I still use today at 70 years of age. It is a miracle piece of equipment. After four months I felt incredibly good, and it was at this time I received a call from Greg Turbill.

Turbs was an ex-Norwood champion and one of the bravest footballers ever to pull on a league guernsey. He played in Norwood premiership sides, and rightfully sits in their hall of fame. On top of this, he was a bloody good bloke. Turbs had been appointed to coach the Moonta Football Club and was into his last season as coach with them. He wanted me to play with Moonta, and phoned me a number of times, and I said no. After about six calls, I finally relented and agreed to play. My body was in excellent shape, and I was 34 years old and still had plenty of football left in me. Moonta is a town situated 165 km northwest of Adelaide and is part of the Copper Triangle, joining Kadina and Wallaroo. The population of Moonta is over 4,000 and it is fondly referred to as "Little Cornwall" because of its rich history, having been settled in 1901.

The idyllic town is located on the shores of Spencer Gulf and Moonta Bay, and makes a pretty picture, drawing many tourists to the area. Moonta Football Club forms part of the Yorke Peninsula Football League and was established in 1896. My ex-Woodville and Richmond teammate Kenny Crane played with the Greek Football Club in Adelaide and invited me to train with them during the week, which I did; and then I would drive up on the Friday and stay the night prior to the game. I was now able to manage my training minus any flog-gings on the track, and always felt a million dollars come game day. Looking back, I could have played another two years of

League Football had my training been managed in an intelligent fashion. The 1986 season was a good one for Moonta, as we made the preliminary final and went down by a point or two. I had an exceptionally good year and for the first time in years really enjoyed my football.

Turbs had decided his body couldn't take any more punishment and reluctantly finished up after the 1986 season. The Club approached me and asked if I would be interested in taking on the coaching job in 1987. I agreed to do the job for one year only. Moonta again played in the finals, but the premiership eluded us again. I had another outstanding year and decided that was it. The travelling was becoming a chore, so now was time to give it away.

I kept my training up and thought that was it as far as football was concerned, until I received a call from Marty Myers. Marty was a liquor salesman and got to travel to areas including Victor Harbour. Like all good salesmen, Marty had a pleasing demeanour and a confident and happy personality. Marty told me that Encounter Bay Football Club were looking for a coach and asked if I would be interested. After a few days I got back to him, and intimated that I would be happy to talk to Encounter Bay and make a decision from there. The next day I got a call from Geoff Stock, the President of Encounter Bay Football Club, and we agreed to meet over lunch at the Apollon Motel in Victor Harbour.

Victor Harbour is a coastal town approximately 85km from Adelaide heading south. The town overlooks the picturesque Encounter Bay. Encounter Bay was named in 1802 by the famous Matthew Flinders. The place is a drawcard for tourists and has a population of roughly 4500 people, and it forms part of the famed Fleurieu Peninsula. It would best be described as a postcard picture place, extremely beautiful with magnificent views. The Encounter Bay Club is over one hundred years old and has a proud history. It is part of the Great Southern Football League which comprises ten teams and is an affiliated member of the South Australian National Football League.

I met with Geoff Stock and Gary Roberts at the Apollon Motor Inn for lunch to discuss the coaching position. Stocky was a very professional man in his fifties and had a relaxing demeanour about him. He was someone you would trust in an instant. Gary was the postmaster in Victor Harbour and was a quiet individual, but very switched on and extremely thorough. Stocky filled me in regarding the Encounter Bay Football Club. Everything about the Club was great, but they hadn't won a premiership for 22 years and the members and supporters were desperate to see another flag. Another premiership before they died, that's how much it meant to them. I asked a lot of questions regarding the players, and in particular about the training methods and frequency, and attendance numbers at training sessions.

After a couple of hours, I told Stocky and Gary that I would be happy to coach the Club and try to win that elusive premiership for them. I added that being 36 years old and a playing coach, three years would definitely see me out and if I couldn't win a flag in that time then I would have to hand the job over to somebody else. I said I would put my heart and soul into the job, but I couldn't give them any more than that. They were both excited and the deal was done. This job was going to be one hell of a challenge and one I looked forward to.

I had a meeting with the players and set out a plan to try and transform the Encounter Bay Football Club into an outfit that opposition sides would fear in terms of physicality, skill, and mental strength. I gave them a training schedule to be done prior to the preseason, and eight football commandments which we would never deviate from on the football field. Each player would live and die by these rules every time he pulled on the Eagles jumper. A training roster was to be kept, and discipline was to be a cornerstone in everything we did. The team attitude was One in, all in. From day one every player knew that only a flag would be viewed as success and there would never be excuses, only encouragement. The eight football rules were to become the steering wheel of this team and the game plan was a basic and easy-to-follow one, where individually and collectively the players knew what was required for every situation that arose in a game.

The players showed up for preseason training in excellent physical condition, so I knew they had adhered to their schedules. I put them through a tough two months of preseason training and was happy with their commitment and attitude. Stocky advised me that the Club had not been able to secure any quality new players and apologised, saying that he did not expect us to make the Grand Final in 1988. I told him not to worry about a thing as I was pleased with the group, and I expected them to do well.

Being a playing coach, there were two important issues to address. One was making sure I did every inch of training shoulder to shoulder with my players, thus gaining their respect and confidence. The other one was to find a good assistant coach. Stocky introduced me to a local dairy farmer named Lenny Russell. Lenny was around the fifty mark and still looked fit. He had been a gun country footballer, playing for Robe in the Mid-Southeast Football League in country South Australia. Lenny was a very affable fellow with a cheeky smile and with the same football philosophies as mine. We were to have three great years together.

1988 was a strong season for the Club, where we unexpectedly made it into the Grand Final, unfortunately going down to Willunga by ten goals. Terrible kicking for goal cost us dearly, as well as my bad decision to play a few boys who were not 100% fit due to injury problems, including myself. No excuses, but lessons learned for another assault on that elusive flag in 1989.

We drowned our sorrows and I took all of the players out onto the ground in the early hours of the morning. I explained to them that the horrible feelings they were all experiencing now would never heal until we won a Premiership and that the upcoming preseason would be hardest they would ever do. I pointed to a huge hill behind the goals and told them there was a light switch at the top, and to get to that switch we would need to win the Premiership and flick it on. The hill would illuminate, and we could then watch all the opposition sides tumble to the bottom of the mountain, and we would stand at the top like kings and bask in the glory. During the 1989 campaign, I would often point to the hill and reinforce the dream. It was a dream all the players embraced.

I asked Stocky to approach David and Andrew Pearson, Lyndon Elsworthy and David Guest, and try to get them on board for the 1989 season. David Pearson was a very talented midfielder with a dynamic left foot, and Andrew was a stoic and determined back pocket player. Lyndon Elsworthy was about 180cm tall, built like a brick shithouse, and was a power-house player who could kick a country mile with either foot and take a big mark. Oigle, as he was known, also had the aggression to go with his other outstanding talents. I had coached these boys at Moonta. David Guest was a big strong ruckman, standing at around 195cm. He could ruck all day and take a big grab and was aggressive and very determined. Guesty had played under 19s football for Carlton. Stocky did a magnificent job in securing all four of these players for the 1989 season.

I had become a marked player in the competition, mainly because of my high profile and because I kicked a lot of goals (103 in 1988 and 127 in 1989). There were a number of players who took filthy cheap shots, and I decided to fight fire with fire. The umpires were a wake-up to what was going on and when I retaliated, most just turned a blind eye. In an exchange with one of these obnoxious individuals, the umpire was only five metres away. In a brief exchange of punches, I dropped him with a short sharp right cross to the jaw.

The umpire looked at me and said, "I've been watching him, Bob, and he has got what he deserved. Just get on with the game now."

I didn't have any more problems with that fellow. After a while I wasn't being bothered as much by blokes trying to knock my head off, as they knew there would be retribution somewhere along the line, either that day or the next game.

There was a bad incident when Encounter Bay played rival Victor Harbour in a Derby at Victor Harbour Oval one day. The Derbys were always fierce contests and there was usually a bit of blood spilt. On this particular day, it was my blood being spilt on the Victor Harbour Oval. There were two brothers playing for Victor Harbor, Rick Searle who had played league football and his brother Mark. Rick was athletic and a good footballer, whilst his brother Mark was more solidly built and a capable footballer. Rick had won possession of the football in Victor's backline, so I gave chase and tackled him to the ground in a fair but hard tackle. I ended up on top of Rick and the quarter time siren sounded to end play.

All of a sudden, Rick started throwing punches into my face while still on his back and then I felt blows striking my face and head from above. The blows from above were being delivered by Mark Searle. After the assault I was bleeding quite heavily from a gash along the top of my eyebrow and had blood all over one side of my face. I walked over to Mark and told him that he would not see this game out today.

Searle told me to get fucked and I responded by saying, "I don't think you understand. I'm telling you that you will not see this game out."

And with that I walked over to my group of players. I asked Lenny to take charge and address the players while I got cleaned up, which he duly did. We had resumed the game and were about ten minutes into the second quarter. Mark Searle was playing on the half back flank and the ball came in high to his area. I took off from full forward making a beeline straight for Searle. I was at absolute top pace and the ball had bounced into the air after hitting the ground, so Searle had turned to track it just as I arrived. My runner Paul Tonkin was only metres away as I whooshed past him, and then thud! I collected Mark Searle right up the middle with the biggest shit-mixer I ever delivered on a football field. He was on the ground and out like a light. He took no further part in the game or the next few games. There was stunned silence at what had just taken place. In fact, not one Victor Harbour player came near me.

After this incident the filthy individuals crawled back into their holes where I was concerned, and I just got on with playing hard but fair football for the rest of my time at the Bays. The 1989 preseason was very solid and as tough as any of these players had ever done. I was very proud of the boys in the way in which each and every one of them had embraced the challenge, and their attitudes were superb. I couldn't have been happier with them. We were as fit as Mallee bulls and ready to start our climb up the mountain to the light switch. We all had the same dream. The side had skill, character, pace, and toughness, and everyone was pulling in the same direction.

Off the ground we had a legendary head trainer in Alan Crispin, who did the work of five people, and he had the medical and massage side running like a well-oiled machine. I had a great runner in Paul Tonkin, a good stats man in Marty Myers, a superb assistant in Lenny Russell, and an administration second to none led by the thorough Geoff Stock.

The Club also had a brilliant group of women who worked tirelessly for the Club raising money, cooking meals and many other tasks. They were led by Marlene Crispin. We blasted into the '89 season and played some dynamic football with our superior fitness showing up time after time; and we were also lucky in the fact injuries were few and far between. Again, we had made the finals and scored ourselves a double chance.

A few days out from the qualifying final, the left side of my face near the jawbone starting to swell dramatically and by the time I got to Flinders Medical Centre the swelling had become the size of a tennis ball. The doctors diagnosed a blocked saliva gland and operated that day. They operated through my mouth and took out what looked like a small white marble. My mouth felt as if a lawnmower had gone through it. The pain was horrible, and I couldn't even swallow my own saliva. While I lay in hospital, Lenny took charge of the side for the qualifying final. If we won it would be a berth straight into the Grand Final and most importantly for me, two weeks to get right. Lose, and we would have to play in the preliminary, which I wouldn't be able to do.

I couldn't talk and could not swallow so I just wrote down a few notes for Lenny, and I knew if anyone could get the job done it was him. We were a very good team and I trusted him fully. I was lying in hospital, feeling extremely miserable. All the hard work and here I was in hospital instead of leading my boys out onto the ground to contest a huge game. At around 6pm, Alicia arrived with the news that the boys had won, and we were into the Grand Final. I was over the moon and the news gave me such a huge lift. I was so proud of Lenny and the boys. I was discharged from hospital the next day and had two weeks to prepare myself and the Club for another tilt at Premiership glory. The Club had been waiting 22 years, and I was hellbent on delivering a flag to them.

I had lost a lot of weight quickly and still had difficulty swallowing, so everything had to be pureed in order for me to be able to get it down—steak, vegetables, pasta, absolutely everything. After about four days of pureed food, I was able to swallow reasonably normally and ate everything I could to get the weight back on. After a week, I was feeling a million dollars and was 7lbs lighter than my normal playing weight. I wasn't able to put the 3kg back on in time for the Grand Final, but it didn't matter as I felt very good and had all of my strength back.

When I caught up with Lenny at training, he was tickled pink with what had transpired and told me he had been shit scared as he didn't want to stuff my side up and knew how big the game was. I had a good laugh, patted him on the back and thanked him for his tremendous effort. My good mate Alan Swain, who played in the reserves that day, relayed news to me of how Lenny had gone during the big day. Swainy divulged that Lenny had smoked a whole packet of cigarettes and at one stage had lit a ciggy not realising that he was already smoking one. Lenny had spoken brilliantly to the boys pre-game; he mentioned the fact their coach was in a hospital bed and powerless to help them and was relying on each of them to get the job done. And get it done they did. I asked Gary Roberts to get me ten Willunga jumpers.

Gazza looked at me and asked, "What the hell do you want those for?"

"Don't worry, Gazza. Just make sure they are here on Tuesday night before training," I replied.

Willunga had beaten us convincingly in the 1988 Grand Final and they were to again play us for the 1989 Premiership. Willunga were a dynamic football club and always had strong teams that barely missed finals action come September. This particular team had a very strong backline who set up many penetrating attacks from the area, combining really well with their mobile brigade. They had pace, skill, and aggression. I had a lot of respect for the Willunga Football Club and still do to this day.

At training I set up a Willunga backline with players wearing the jumpers Gary Roberts had procured. Although the players didn't know it, the forward line was set up the way we would start in the Grand Final on Saturday. The ball was pumped deep into the forward line time after time and all forwards put tremendous heat on anything in a Willunga jumper, smothering the effectiveness of kicks and handballs at every given opportunity. The idea was to create panic so that everything they did was rushed, thus leading to mistakes and more opportunities for us.

The final training session was conducted on Thursday and the boys looked very sharp and strong. Bring on Saturday. I had a full, fit and healthy list of players raring to go, with no one under an injury cloud as was the case in 1988. Saturday arrived, a beautiful clear sunny day with little wind and the smell of freshly cut turf wafting in the air. There was a packed house, with the air of tension and excitement reigning supreme. What more could a footballer ask for?

Our reserves were also in the Grand Final. They were led by the B grade coach Arch Harding, a stalwart of the Club and a very good ruckman who had given his heart and soul to the Bays. Arch and his boys played a blinder and got over the line to win a B Grade flag for Encounter Bay, a tremendous effort. The scene had been set and now it was our turn to have a crack. Ten minutes prior to the game, I deliberately left the players seated in a room on their own. I left them there for a few minutes then walked in. There was plenty of noise in the room and a lot of nervous tension. I spoke to them in a calm manner to bring the tension down, and mentioned our dream and how lucky we all were to have this opportunity and not to waste a second of it.

"The ball is the only priority," I said, "and giving away stupid undisciplined free kicks would not be tolerated. We have the chance to do something tremendous today and it is one in, all in. Look after each other at all costs and stay focused on our system."

With that, out we went. The first quarter was fierce and by quarter time there was nothing in the game. It was very tight. I wasn't happy with the lack of pressure on the Willunga back-line, and addressed this plus a couple of other small issues. The boys exploded into action at the start of the second quarter and ramped up the pressure and aggression levels to maximum. We threw everything at Willunga and the cracks started to show. By half time, after a quarter of this plus some exhilarating football, we found ourselves up by ten goals. It was unbelievable but we had another half to go and needed to keep absolutely focused and not relax for one second. Willunga came back at us and got within five goals, but we pulled away again and won the game by ten goals.

The Bay supporters went nuts and to witness so many ecstatic joyous happy faces was a very moving moment. As for me, I felt a huge surge of relief and a contentment which I had rarely experienced. A job I gave myself three years to achieve had been done in two. We celebrated for a whole week and basked in the glory of what we had done. The mountain had been conquered and the light switch flicked on. What a view from the top! Glorious.

My ex-Fitzroy coach Billy Stephen had organised five VFL Grand Final tickets for me; he had sold off the Finals series tickets and kept the Grand Final ones. Five of us attended the 1989 VFL Grand Final between Hawthorn and Geelong, and this was to be the first of many for our group of five. Ash took his four-wheel drive and he did all of the driving—something he loved to do, drive and smoke. The rest of us drank and had a jolly old time. Leigh Andrewartha, Swainy, and I sat in the back and another good mate, Roger Donhart, was in the front with Ash. Leigh had played a lot of country football and told us that he was pretty good. I told him that if I was his coach, I'd put him in the middle so that he could tear the game apart and dominate, become the dominator; from this I called him "Dommy" and that is his nickname even today. We all met at the tollgate situated at the bottom of the Adelaide Hills at around 7:30 am on the Thursday, and off we went. The first beer was cracked open by 7:40 am and we drank all the way to Melbourne, stopping at Horsham for a big lunch and arriving in Melbourne in time to watch one of the sides train.

Ash got on his CB radio and talked to the truckies heading towards Adelaide from Melbourne, trying to get information on radar positions. He was in his element, and you would think he had been driving trucks for years, he was that good at it. The truckies relayed all the radar traps to him—very useful information. Ash would ask the truckie if there were any blue pineapples around and all sorts of truckie talk would take place. Watch out for the town clown (local police) or hairdryer (radar set up), plain wrapper (unmarked police car), Evil Knievel (cop on a bike), and on it would go.

After a few hours of this the boys wanted some music as by now they'd had enough truckie talk. But except for one time when he played some Elvis songs, Ash would not relent as he didn't want a speeding ticket. Within 30 minutes of putting on the music we got done for speeding. While Ash was sorting out the fine the boys took the opportunity to have a piss. Ash was furious with getting a ticket, so we all agreed to chip in to cover the fine. We got on with having a good time but minus the music; no more music and no more fines.

Dommy would smoke a couple of joints in the back and swirl the smoke around Roger's head in the front passenger seat. Ash had the windshield on his side so his window was always open to facilitate his continuous smoking, and the smoke from the joint didn't affect him at all. As for Roger, he may as well have been smoking the joint. Roger hadn't drunk as nearly as much beer as Swainy, Dommy, or me; but on this occasion when we arrived in Melbourne he was smashed, plastered, stewed. He was a very wonky little Roger indeed, and he couldn't work out what the hell had happened to him.

Dommy eventually explained it to him and added, "Surely you could smell the smoke, cunt." He used this word when referring to his good mates but rarely used it in general conversation. Roger brushed it off and it was the last time he ever sat in the front passenger seat on our future trips to Melbourne. We would take Billy out to a long lunch on the Friday and then present him with a decent gift, go to the Grand Final on Saturday, then to the Boundary Hotel after the game, and on to our favourite Chinese restaurant in Little Bourke Street at around 8:30pm. We got to know the Chinese owner really well over the years and he would certainly look after us. After a huge Saturday, we would head back to Adelaide on Sunday morning and have a big session on the way home.

Alicia was invariably in a pissed-off mood when I got home, and this would make the boys a big edgy or uncomfortable and in turn would make me feel angry, but I tried not to show it. She would do this sort of shit quite often. Most times when the boys left, the behaviour would lead to an argument, which left me feeling really down. I was growing so tired of her manipulative ways and felt like just walking out many times, but couldn't bear the thought of walking out on my children. Just the thought of it made me feel so sad. At times I felt so hopelessly trapped and very unhappy.

I had one more year to go with Encounter Bay, so I set about planning the 1990 season. I lost around eight players from the 1989 side due to them having work commitments and moving, plus a couple of retirements, etc. 1990 was going to be difficult so I decided to blood young players and do the best I could with the side we had. I had another clean-up operation on my right knee during the 1990 season, the fourth such operation during my playing career, and missed five or six games. The side made the Finals, but we couldn't go on with it and bombed out.

My time as a player had come to an end at 38 years of age and I had nothing to complain about. It was a terrific run. I did feel extreme sadness that I would never pull the boots on again, but I also felt relief that I would never, ever have to do another preseason. Three great years with Encounter Bay FC was a good way to finish my football career and now it was on to the next phase of life, albeit without football.

I became very good friends with Wayne Rodrigues who was a manager with HUFF Freight in Adelaide. Wayne organised our freight as we sent bingo and beer tickets all over the State. I got on well with him from the first meeting we had at Mile End on the footpath outside our printer's premises on Richmond Road. Wayno was a very affable happy-go-lucky bloke, and we had two things in common, one being football and the other a love of Elvis Presley. Wayne was a good singer and at one stage had his own band. He would bring his wife and kids over for a meal and Alicia and I would go to his house now and again.

One night at around 6pm there was a knock on the front door and standing there was Wayne. He had a sad look on his face and when we sat down at the kitchen table, Wayne broke down in tears. He explained that his wife had walked out on him and gone off with another bloke. The worst part was that Wayne had a couple of young kids, and his wife flew the coop anyhow. I put my arm around Wayne and tried the best I could to console him while Alicia made a coffee. We talked for a couple of hours and then he left. I'm sure he felt sad and empty inside, but he was better for the talk. Wayne battled through and ended up meeting a lovely lady called Cathy, and they are still together today, some 30 years on. Wayne's ex-wife left the dropkick she had run off with as he had started to physically abuse her in quite a bad way. I still keep in contact with Wayne and Cathy, who have become lifelong friends.

In early April 1992, I received a shattering phone call from David Guest, my Premiership ruckman from the 1989 Premiership side. Guesty was sobbing on the phone, and was heartbroken as he told me that David Pearson, another player from the '89 side, was dead. I had to ask Guesty to repeat himself and he explained through huge emotion that Pearso had been killed in a head-on crash on the Goolwa Road at Middleton, not far out of Victor Harbour. David's partner Sue and another young woman had also been killed in the crash. The only survivor was Pearso's teammate and former North Adelaide league footballer Paul Zoontjens. What a rotten, sad day.

David Pearson's parents John and Jan asked me to do the eulogy for their son, which I agreed to do. I did the eulogy in the Encounter Bay Football Club with Pearso's coffin right alongside me. This was one of the hardest tasks I have had to complete in my life. The emotion was unbearable and over-whelming. John asked me to write out the eulogy for him as he wanted to frame it and put it on his wall, and when I got home, I wrote it out and posted it to him. Years later, John asked me how I could possibly write something like that; it made him feel so proud of his son. I told him David meant a lot to me and I tried to do the best for him with the eulogy, as he was a cham-pion bloke and a champion footballer.

In 1992, Adelaide Fundraising Supplies had been operating for over ten years. I had set up a very small contract cleaning business and was keen to pursue the venture. Ash was keen to keep operating the ticket business, so we decided to go our separate ways as far as business was concerned. Ash paid me out my share of Adelaide Fundraising Supplies and I concentrated on developing A&B Commercial Cleaning Services, but first I decided to take Alicia on a four-week trip to America. Mum and Dad were to come over from West Australia and look after Tanya, Brett and Aaron while we were away.

In October of 1992 we jetted off to America and it was all very exciting. Mum was very worried about Alicia and I going to America as, like most people back in Australia, all she ever heard about the place was gloom and doom, mountains of murderers and violence, all delivered by the news services.

Maria would say, "Why you want to go to America, son? You will be hilled (killed). Look at da news, no good."

I would just say, "For god's sake, Mum, do you really believe all of that crap? I have spoken to people who have been, and they all love the place; they reckon our press in Australia need a kick up the arse for the shit they get away with. Please don't believe the rubbish they throw at you, it's all sensationalist bullshit."

"You tink so, son," she would reply, and finish off with, "You be hareful, son."

We flew out to Los Angeles and visited many of the tourist places on the west coast. We went to Memphis to see Graceland, the home of Elvis Presley, which I was enthralled with; then Grand Canyon, Las Vegas, San Antonio, San Francisco, Orlando, Louisiana, and many more places. I never saw any violence and felt far safer walking around America than I did back in Australia. I loved talking to the people, who were very friendly and helpful and had a certain energy or vibe about them. Everything about this great country impressed me, although I thought they ate too much.

I soon came to the realisation that Australians were being fed a diet of sensationalist rubbish by the press, and to this day I believe little of what they print or show to their citizens. In fact, more than ever the press needs to be controlled. Yes, some of what they say is true, but a lot is not.

Alicia contacted the kids every couple of days, and I would also talk to them and to Mum. Dad would rarely get on the phone. The kids were starting to whine to Alicia about everything, stuff like: we hate her food, and she is too strict with us and she drinks too much. She would have a couple of drinks at night with Dad. Alicia didn't drink, so I understood the drinking bit. But instead of telling the kids to pull their heads in, Alicia would side with them, enable them, and say, "I will fix everything when I get home." She then referred to my mother as "Nanny Goat Boozer".

Alicia had become super-possessive of Tanya, Brett, and Aaron, and created a situation of her and the kids against me, my mother and father, or anyone else for that matter. If I dared discipline the children, all hell would break loose, which made me feel like a sperm donor, not the father. She was undermining me constantly where the kids were concerned, and I really started to feel and see it. Alicia was starting to get moody after a couple of weeks into the trip, wanting to get back to Hallett Cove to save her children from Nanny Goat Boozer, and it was starting to impact on what was supposed to be an adventure of a lifetime. I was determined to soldier on and have a good time, knowing this might be the only opportunity I would have of seeing this magnificent country.

We stayed in Louisiana for five days and booked into a hotel in New Orleans, not very far from Bourbon Street, which is a historic street located in the French Quarter. Bourbon Street really comes to life at night, pumping with all kinds of live music, and heaps of little restaurants and bars giving off a full-on party atmosphere and exciting energy. Just being there makes one feel alive and happy. There was an abundance of interesting characters and people wandering around drinking all sorts of alcoholic concoctions from plastic cups, as drinking in this street is permitted. I found the place intoxicating and loved the vibe; it didn't take long to get into the swing of Bourbon Street.

During our second night there, Alicia and I went looking for a place to have dinner. We had eaten at a Cajun restaurant the night before and the food was exemplary. Alicia didn't like the waiter, an Afro-American in his early 60s whom I thought represented what New Orleans was all about. He was a character in every sense of the word and had a good personality, almost as if he had stepped out of a movie set and into this little restaurant, and I was keen to go back there to have another meal. Alicia kicked up a stink and refused point blank to go back there, and I told her to select a restaurant so that we could eat. We wandered all over the place and Alicia couldn't make up her mind; she was also starting to get narky. Me, I was getting hungry and tired of traipsing around looking for a place to eat. There were so many and here we were still looking after an hour.

In the end I told Alicia that I was going back to the little Cajun restaurant we had eaten at the previous evening. Alicia decided to come with me but she was in one of her shit moods by this stage and I knew the night would only get worse, because when she got into these moods being with her was horrible. Alicia liked to make me feel horrible, and not just for a night; it could take anywhere from two to five days for her to snap out of it. We sat down and ate a beautiful Cajun meal then started to walk down Bourbon Street.

Alicia was well into her foul mood by this stage, so I just stopped and reminded her that this was a trip of a lifetime, and I was going to enjoy the experience. It was a long way from home and what's more it had cost a lot of money, and I wanted to remember it as a happy, exciting experience. It was always pointless even speaking with Alicia when she was in one of her moods, as it would end up in an angry argument and the bad mood index would go into the red zone. She told me to go forth and multiply and stormed back to the hotel. I wandered around listening to the music and knocking back a few beverages. In one of the bars a fellow and his wife started talking to me. He was a cop from New York, an interesting bloke with a happy persona. When he introduced himself, he said, "I'm a cop with the NYPD and a damn good one." I spent a couple of hours with them and had a good time, then wandered off to another bar.

The time had flown and looking at my watch I was surprised to see it was now 2 am. I set off for the walk back to the hotel and on nearing my destination came across a bar that was noisy and vibrant. I walked in, sat at the bar and ordered a dark rum and Coke. A beautiful-looking woman sat down alongside me and introduced herself as Dianne, and started talking to me. She was strikingly attractive and appeared to be very intelligent, and had an easygoing personality. After about ten minutes I turned and gazed around the place, especially the dance floor. To my horror I saw blokes dancing and kissing each other and women doing the same. My god, I was in a bloody gay bar! I turned to Diane and told her I was not gay and that I knew she was a bloke, and I had to be on my way. Diane tried to convince me that she was not a bloke but to no avail. She followed me out onto the street and said, "Honey, I love the way you fill those jeans out." She gave me her phone number and told me if ever I came back to please give her a call. I bade Diane farewell and bolted back to the hotel. I had experienced some sort of night and had a good time. The trip, and what America was about, had really opened my eyes. It was a terrific place with friendly people.

I loved it but now it was back to South Australia and on with life, whatever it had in store. We arrived back home to Hallett Cove, and it didn't take long for things to turn into a clusterfucking Charlie Foxtrot. No sooner had we put our bags down than the kids were all over Alicia exposing all of their terrible woes under the leadership of that horrible Nanny Goat Boozer, and just how horrible their little lives had been for five weeks under this tyrant. Alicia lapped it up quicker than a puppy drinking its egg and milk. She verbally laid into Mum and literally had fire emanating out of her nostrils.

I told Alicia to be quiet and pull her head in and that she should respect my parents as they had travelled all the way from WA to look after the children, and as far as I could see they looked perfectly fine. This had no effect and Alicia kept on. Then Dad erupted and let loose on Tanya, whom he considered the troublemaker, bearing in mind that Tanya was no child by this stage, but a young adult. I then turned to Alicia and angrily told her she should be ashamed of herself and how dare she treat my mother and father in this manner.

I went to Mum and Dad and divulged my disgust at what had just occurred, and assured them that everything would be okay. Mum and Dad left a couple of days later and I could see they were very upset. Alicia's manipulation concerning the children meant that they would have little to do with their grandparents ever again. After my parents left, I let Alicia have it. I told her I was sick and tired of the way she had turned my own children against me, and now she had done the same with my mother and father. I said that as far as I was concerned, Alicia had been brainwashing Tanya, Brett and Aaron since the day they were born and I was just a sperm donor, not their father, and through manipulation she had created a situation of her and the kids against me. I told her I was fed up with her undermining me continually where the children were concerned. I also emphasised how her lies and extremely jealous ways were getting hard to live with. Alicia had made up so many lies about other women, particularly if they were attractive. She would say things like: "Oh, so and so thinks you are a real prick, she hates you". I had believed this bullshit for many years and did not speak to the people concerned. Alicia just denied the lot, and it was a waste of time even venting my frustrations to her. Looking back, I consider myself to have been a total idiot, and an absolute numbskull for getting sucked in. I still find it hard to comprehend to this day.

We soldiered on with A&B Commercial Cleaning Services. The work was very solid and there was little time for distractions. Alicia, I will give her her due, was a very hard worker and worked tirelessly alongside me in the business. The venture went on for seven years. We had some solid contracts, and the business was very labour-intensive. At one stage we would work from 4:30pm to 7pm, then from 10pm through to 6am in the morning. After a while we scaled the business back and worked 4:30pm to7pm and then got up at 3am and worked through to 6:30 or 7am. The work was tough, but the money was good and we got used to the nature of it all.

I had all day free, so I decided to take on a job reading power meters in the hilly Blackwood area and its surroundings. Chris was the boss and had his own subcontracting business reading the meters for ETSA, the Electricity Trust of south Australia. I met with Chris, and he told me there was only one area left, which was Blackwood. Chris was a good fellow and made me feel comfortable from the outset. He was one of those blokes that everyone likes, and he went out of his way to make sure you were okay. You could sense that he genuinely cared about people.

He recoiled into his chair and gave out a sigh. "Mate, I've got to be totally honest with you. Blackwood is a prick of an area where meter reading is concerned. It is very hilly and full of savage dogs. It has a no-read rate of 45% and blokes only last a couple of weeks up there, and that is why it is available. If you want to take it on it's yours, but I need you to understand how difficult it will be. I don't want you to come back and abuse or thump me for not filling you in." There was a moment's silence then he said, "And what's more, you'll be walking anywhere up to six or seven hours a day, depending on the run, through some bloody hilly country. Some runs may only take five hours, but it is an area that no one wants to work. What do you think?"

I was up for the challenge and agreed to take the job on. Chris was excited and said, "I can see you are more than fit enough, but mate, watch out for the bloody dogs. I'll start teaching you about the reading side on Monday."

That was it; a week of training and I was into it. Rarely a day would go by where I wasn't involved in an altercation with a savage dog, so much so that I armed myself with a waddy. The waddy was 550mm long made with 10mm reinforced tubular steel covered with poly pipe and fitted with a wooden handle which was then covered with a bike handle grip. It was solid, and I could move it quickly. I love dogs to bits, but the dogs I'm talking about were very vicious and wanted to tear me to shreds. It was most of the owners I should have taken to with the waddy. No matter how many precautions I took, I got nailed a fair few times; but the waddy at least gave me a chance to get out unscathed. Some days I would walk into the office after my run and have torn shorts and dried blood trails on my legs and Chris would want to hear the story. Although the attacks were serious, Chris and I would end up having a good laugh about the event.

One day I went to open a Colorbond gate leading into a yard. Both owners were standing in the yard, so I thought nothing of it. I opened the gate and all of a sudden, a red heeler came at me like a bat out of hell, so I shut the gate in its face. But unbeknown to me there was a loose piece of tin on the gate, and the dog's head went straight through and he chomped into my right leg, halfway between the knee and ankle. It was a hot day and I had been walking for hours. The blood poured out and I vented my anger directly at the owners.

"I am sick and tired of people like you and your fucking dogs," I told the two of them. "I'm not going to report you because you will lose your dog, or worse, it will be put down. But be warned, next time I come back and your dog attacks me I will defend myself forcefully. Now get me some fucking antiseptic."

The couple were in their mid-forties and the male shouted at his partner to get some Dettol, which I poured over the wound and then bandaged it. I always carried a roll of cotton bandaging just in case of a snake bite or dog attack. When I was leaving, I looked at the male and told him to remember what I said about the dogs and that I would be back in three months.

Around 30 minutes later, a police car pulled up alongside me and the copper asked me why I was carrying the waddy, which was tucked into my belt. I pointed to my leg and told him about the dog problems I encountered nearly every day. He fully understood and enquired which house this attack occurred at. I flicked back through my reading device and gave him the details.

A worried look appeared on his face, and he said, "Shit, mate, they're a bad lot that live in that house. We are there all the time; they are bloody feral."

He told me to take care and to make sure I reported the attack, and was then on his way. I didn't report the attack, but I learnt to work smarter where dogs were concerned, and got to know the area very well. It was my patch. I had a tetanus booster before taking on the job, so that was one thing I didn't have to worry about.

Three months later, I was back at the same house and pulled the waddy from my belt and entered the yard to read the meter. A few paces in and the dog flew out of the laundry and attacked. I let rip with some heavy blows into the dog's ribs, both sides, and after about four of these the dog yelped and retreated to the laundry. A young male of around 20 appeared and before he could say anything I ripped into him about his dog and what had happened the last time. He just stood there and didn't say anything. I turned and walked onto the next property. I never had a problem with that particular dog again. It was always locked in the laundry whenever I ventured in to read the meter.

After a year, the dog attacks were happening less and less, as I got to know the patch like the back of my hand. And I had got the no-read ratio down to just 5%. Chris was over the moon with this, and I was happy to be able to do the job for him.

But no matter how smart and careful I was where dogs were concerned, I would still get nailed on the odd occasion. One such time was with a big Alsatian. It was a beautiful-looking dog but it was very protective of the owner, a lady in her 50s. She had two Alsatians and I would yell out to her before entering the yard, and she would grab the dogs and yell out for me to enter. I would yell back, "Have you got both dogs under control?" The answer was always yes. The meter was only two paces inside the gate, so I would enter and hastily do the reading, then retreat and shout out, "All good—I have finished!" No sooner had I shut the gate than the dogs would tear around the corner of the house and hit the gate in a menacing mood.

On one particular visit to this house, I went through the same protocol and then entered, read the meter and turned to leave. I heard the woman shriek, "Oh shit!" And by the time I had my hand on the gate and turned to my left, it was too late. The big dog came at full pelt and bit my left thigh. The woman was screaming at the dog, which possibly saved me from a few more bites, and I managed to get out through the gate.

"I thought you had that bloody dog under control. What the hell were you doing?"

"I'm so sorry! He broke my grip. Are you okay?" she asked.

"I will be when I clean my leg up. I need antiseptic. Do you think you can get me some?" She came back with antiseptic and warm water. I cleaned and bandaged the wound, then told her I wouldn't be reporting the attack.

"I know how much you love your dog," I said, "and it's not the dog's fault. But it had better not happen again as I won't be so forgiving the next time. So when I come in the future, you'll need to tie them up or put both dogs inside." The lady understood and thanked me for not reporting her dog and I went on my way.

I got to know a lot of the residents on my run, and some of them were old ladies living on their own. Some would ask me to lift certain things for them, move the odd items like flowerpots or furniture around, tighten up loose brackets, etc. They would be little jobs which only took a couple of minutes and I was always happy to oblige even though in that job time was of the essence. A lot of the little old ladies looked forward to my visits and would offer tea or coffee, but I had to keep moving so would have a quick chat and keep going.

They appeared to be very lonely, and I felt so sorry for them. In one of the houses, I came across an old lady huddled in her kitchen with a blanket wrapped around her and all of the lights switched off. I found my way to the meter using my torch, and then asked her why she was sitting in the dark. The poor dear told me she could not afford to pay for the electricity, so rugged up to keep warm and left the lights off. What sort of human being would let a member of their family live this way?

On the next visit to this house, I saw a chap outside who appeared to be about 45 years old, maybe 50, and I asked him where the old lady was. He told me he was her son and that his mother had passed away three days ago. I told him I was sorry to hear that as his mother was such a nice lady. What the son needed was a swift kick up the arse for the pain that poor old lady had to endure. But as much as I would have liked to let him know how I felt, it was a lose-lose situation, so I was better off letting karma deal with this one.

It was a reasonably hot day in November 1996, and I was driving back to the office after finishing my run up in the Blackwood area. I pulled up at the lights controlling the inter-section of Richmond and Main South Roads, which was usually a fairly busy intersection, but on this particular day at 4pm it was reasonably quiet. Whilst waiting for the lights to change, a bikie pulled up right next to me on my side. He was on a Harley and had his colours on plus a big chain and padlock draped across his right shoulder and chest, and he wore a German cut-off style helmet. To this day I couldn't say what gang he represented as I never focused on his bikie vest.

Just as the lights changed, the animal leant down and spat in my face, just like that, for no reason at all. I could not believe what had just taken place. I went to get out of my car, but the lights changed and he went. I had a roo bar on my Subaru and made up my mind to chase the piece of garbage and knock him off his bike. My blood was boiling. I was in a rage and any semblance of self-control had completely vanished. To my surprise, the bikie was so brazen and cocksure of himself that he pulled into the BP service station over the road. He pulled up near the entry to the shop and I parked up right in front of the shop entry. I threw my glasses on the passenger seat and got out of the car.

I walked straight up to the bikie and said, "What's your fucking problem?"

He pushed me in the chest and told me I was a cock sucker. I smacked him right on the nose with three short sharp lefts and then unloaded with a big right into the left side of his jaw. Had he not had his helmet on, this fellow would have been asleep, as I had hit half his helmet and half of his jaw at the same time, in the process damaging my little finger. The force knocked him back five or six metres, and he then took his helmet off and threw it into the concrete. The helmet bounced into the air like a ball. In he came swinging. I blocked his roundhouse right and put my left forearm across the back of his neck and pushed down, then drove half a dozen big uppercuts square into his face. The bikie was furiously driving his right knee up and down in a desperate attempt at connecting with my balls. I had turned my body to my right, trying to get as much power into the uppercuts as possible. His knee was just sliding up and down my left thigh but after about half a dozen of these hits, his knee stopped moving. I gave him a few more for good measure then just pushed him away.

People at the bowsers had all frozen as if time had stood still, and the two shop girls ran out and screamed at me to stop. I had stopped and I told them that no piece of bikie shit was going to spit in my face and get away with it. The bikie was bleeding profusely from his face and had blood coming out of his mouth and didn't know what day it was. I could have easily laid into him again and put the piece of filth into a hospital bed, but he didn't have any fight left in him and he would be sore and sorry for a while. My shirt was ripped, and I had his blood on my singlet; other than that, nothing.

I drove off and went back to the office. I wondered if the bikie got my rego number. He obviously didn't, otherwise the rest of them would have come after me. Or maybe they would have told him he was a fool and given him another belting for bringing unwanted attention to the gang. Who knows.

Chris thought I had been done over by the dogs again. I told him what had happened, and he patted me on the back and said, "Bloody well done, mate. You should have run over the bike as well." I was 44 years old and hoped this would be the last time I would have to fight.

Being only ten minutes from McLarenvale was ideal and I would buy wine and store it in the cellar at home. I purchased a forty-litre oak barrel and placed it down in the cellar. The barrel was filled with two twenty-litre cartons of cheap ruby port from the Vales, and then blended with a special mixture consisting of one litre of the ruby, four cinnamon sticks, and a small amount of marsala. The mixture would be left for a week then strained and added into the barrel, and the port would sit there for a few months. The end product was magnificent, and my mates couldn't get enough of it after a meal. As the cellar was under the dining area, it wasn't far to go to refill the litre clay crock bottle, which I would do a few times after a good meal. The boys loved this port so much that they referred to it as Angel's Piss.

I also had a lot of home brew in the cellar, ranging from draught beer to pale ales and stout, and even nut-brown ale. All of them were very good quality, as brewing the stuff became a hobby of mine. A typically good night would consist of downing copious amounts of home brew followed by a beautiful meal. Meals were always superb as Alicia was a magnificent cook. She could cook anything and everything and it was always five star. After the meal it would be down into the cellar again and fill the crock with port. We would venture out to the patio for a cigar, then back inside for a night of frivolity. I really loved this part of life and had many a good time at Hallett Cove with friends.

A good friend of mine whom I met at the Hallett Cove Tavern was Roscoe, a tall thinly-built bloke who looked a lot like Nick Cave, the singer. Roscoe drove trucks for a living and had a gentle personality and also a lot of intelligence. I would catch up with him on the odd Friday night for a few beers, and it was on one of these nights that he asked me if I wanted to go fishing with him and a couple of mates. We arranged to go on a Sunday morning and planned to head down the coastline towards Aldinga in Roscoe's boat.

The full esky was loaded onto the boat plus all our fishing gear, and off we went at around 8:30 in the morning. It was a beautiful warm sunny day; the ocean was flat, and the water sparkled like a blue crown jewel. As we cut along the coastline heading towards Christie's beach, I happened to ask Roscoe where we would be throwing the lines in.

He looked at me with a big smile and beamed. "Fuck the fishing, mate. Worry about that later, because right now we are heading to Maslin to drink some piss and observe scenery."

Maslin was a nudist beach which I had only heard about but never actually visited. We anchored the boat about 30 metres from shore and floated the esky to the beach. We all wore footy shorts and took up a spot on the sand. I had no interest in removing my shorts and nor did the boys. It was a very interesting couple of hours spent there, with all types of bodies parading around in the nude. A few, like us, had shorts or budgie smugglers on and the ages ranged from people in their twenties to some in their eighties. It all seemed so normal, but in all honesty some of it was pure visual pollution which needed to be covered up.

We jumped back into the boat and headed to another beach and pulled in for a few more beers before heading to Christies Beach. Once there, we tied up at the jetty and walked to the Christies Beach Hotel for a meal and to purchase a slab of Victorian Bitter. We pulled away from the jetty at around 3:30 in the afternoon and headed back to Hallett Cove, and as we neared the oil refinery at Lonsdale, Roscoe suggested we throw a line in as it was reputed to be a good fishing spot.

"Well, boys, someone had better catch a fish. I mean, what are we going to tell the women?"

And with that, Roscoe brought the boat to a halt and we threw our lines in. Around ten minutes later, I felt a huge tug on my line and started to pull it up. Whatever was on the end of it was strong. What was on the end of the line was a small shark, just over one metre long. We got it into the boat and headed off home. The light had faded and by the time we got back to my place at Olivier Terrace, Hallett Cove, it was dark. Roscoe gave a spiel to the women explaining how we had fished our guts out all day and this was all we had to show for it. The look of disappointment was etched across his face.

I have no idea what the women thought but Roscoe had a way of making even the biggest sceptic swallow whatever he delivered. I dragged the shark along, cleaned it and cut the thing up so we could freeze most of it. When the time came to eat the shark, it turned out to be superb. We had a good meal and washed it all down with coffee and a few ports. The day was done, and a good time had by all. Now it was off to bed and ready for another grinding week.

Tanya had decided to join the Air Force but first she had to get fit enough to get through the induction, the physical part of it. Tanya had grown into a very attractive young lady and had the most beautiful brown eyes I have ever seen, auburn hair and a lovely figure. She also had olive skin, inherited from her mum. Tanya asked me if I could train her up to a level so that she could get through the induction, which of course I agreed to do. She was a very intelligent girl, but training was not her forte. I set out a programme and designated days to do the work, which would be done over a period of 6-8 weeks.

She got stuck into the program but there were many times when she screamed at me, "I'm not going to do it anymore. I'm fucking going home!" Tanya wasn't one to swear but the training made her feisty and, on these occasions, I would have to grab her by the arm and reiterate why we were here and ask her how badly she wanted to join the Air Force. Did she want to pass this physical or not? Tanya would look at me and not utter a word and then we would be back into it. I would give her a pat on the back and tell her how well she was doing. She had a nice running style and covered the ground well, particularly in the quarter mile and 200-metre runs. We got to the end of the program, and I was very proud of her. She was chuffed and ended up breezing through the induction.

Tanya chose to partake in the nursing side of the Air Force and later became an accomplished nursing sister, working in orthopaedics and the heart ward after leaving the Air Force. Whilst in the Force, Tanya met a young officer, Michael Leahy. Mike was very fit and extremely intelligent. He had impeccable manners and was involved in training fighter pilots. He was easy to be around and knew exactly where he was heading. After a while, Tanya and Michael decided to get married. Alicia and I hired a big hall overlooking Hallett Cove and we decided to do all the catering and setting up of the hall for the reception. It was a huge job. The hall was roughly 800 metres from home and the Catholic Church was the same.

The guest list totalled just over one hundred people and the cost would be approximately $4,000, which was reasonably cheap because we were doing all the work ourselves. We enlisted a few neighbours to give us a hand. Steve and Julie Myer, Steve and Marissa Crouch and a couple of others were all a great help, which we really appreciated. I borrowed all the tables and chairs, plus cutlery, from the South Adelaide Football Club, which was one of our cleaning contracts. Brian Ploenges was the Manager and a top bloke so that made things a lot easier.

The hall was set up and we decorated it with balloons and streamers. The place looked an absolute treat. I had one Weber kettle BBQ and managed to borrow five more, and with these we cooked butts of beef and turkeys under the patio near the pool. All the meat, salads and sweets were made at home and taken up to the hall a couple of hours before the reception.

Tanya looked a picture, and it was off to the church. She, of course, was very nervous. The church service went like clock-work and then off we went to do the photos which seemed to take an eternity. But in the end it was worth the time as they turned out to be first class. Michael came from a large family and his mother, father, and sister had driven over from Victoria. We all rocked up to the hall and got on with the reception. It turned out to be a wonderful night and the food was a big hit with the guests. The celebrations wound up at around midnight and then it was into cleaning up the hall. I will always remember what a huge job that was. We really appreciated the help we got from Steve Myer and a couple of mates. By the time the job had been completed it was 6:30am. I flopped into bed and didn't wake up until two o'clock in the afternoon.

Michael and Tanya were based at Edinburgh, the RAAF Air Force base in South Australia, located roughly 20 km north of Adelaide. On several occasions when Michael and Tanya visited us at Hallett Cove, Mike and I would go on a run with our German Shepherd, Shredder. She was a beautiful big female Shepherd, and she and I did this particular run three times per week. The run was approximately six kilometres, but because of the three big flights of steps at the cliff and hilly nature of Hallett Cove, the run was quite taxing. Mike was young and fit and handled the run really well. I often thought he was a credit to the Air Force and if his colleagues were like him—and most of them were—then Australia could be very proud of their military men and women.

After a while, Tanya started to struggle with Air Force life and was on the phone to Alicia constantly, complaining about the bullying and being left on her own a lot as Michael was often away on exercises. I spoke to Tanya on a few occasions but anything I said just did not seem to help as she appeared to get more and more depressed. As well as Tanya, Alicia also spent a lot of time on the phone with Michael, but the relationship appeared to be heading south. After speaking at length with Michael, I could see he was trying everything to make Tanya happy, but to no avail. Tanya could swing into terrible moods at times and nothing you said or did would bring her out of them. Basically you would just have to wait for her to come out of it, and sometimes it could take days. I knew exactly what Mike was going through but felt powerless to help.

Looking back, I would be the worst bloke to help out in relationship woes. God knows I had enough problems dealing with my own marriage. Sadly, Tanya and Michael separated and eventually divorced. I felt very sad about the whole affair as Michael was a standout person, one in a million, and I just could not get my head around the failure of this relationship. I hope one day Tanya will be able to sit down and explain it to me. She threw herself into nursing and became very good at it. She was happy to be out of the Air Force and appeared to settle down, although the little moody periods still surfaced occasionally.

I have a vivid memory of Tanya and I being the only ones left in the house waiting to be picked up and taken to the church for her wedding. We were standing near the breakfast bar in the kitchen, and I looked directly at her and asked, "Are you sure, Tanya, that you want to do this? There is still time to pull out."

Her answer floored me, as she replied, "I'm not sure."

Gazing into her eyes, I explained, "Tanya, for Christ's sake, you need to be certain that you want to do this. Stuff the church and reception if you don't want to go ahead. That's okay. Make sure of your decision. Do you want to go ahead and get married?" There was a pause, and in hindsight, right there and then I don't think Tanya really wanted to get married.

Alicia started to stack on the weight and didn't care too much about it. She would be into the fridge at two in the morning and speaking to her about it would start an argument. The last thing I wanted was another argument and the shit mood that followed.

I had become President of the Hallett Cove Tavern Social Club; we would get the place really buzzing on a Friday night and raked in a lot of money with our raffles. All the Social Club members would be issued with a couple of tickets and during the night we would announce that all social club members were entitled to a free schooner. It didn't take long to recruit new members. The publican was ecstatic with the Social Club, and we were happy to run a solid club.

The club would throw the odd picnic during the year, but the biggest event was the Christmas function held in a beautiful little park not far from the tavern. We would have our own Father Christmas who delivered gifts to all the members' children. The gifts were good quality and reasonably expensive. After the gifts were handed to every child, it was into the BBQ and some games, such as sack races and so on. It was always a fantastic day enjoyed by both the adults and children.

The tavern was always a source of entertainment. There was not a lot of trouble, but if there was it was usually outsiders that caused it. It was around 9:30 pm one Friday and the bar had emptied out with only 20-25 patrons left. I was having a beer with my mate Steve Arnold, who worked for Telecom and was a local. We both glanced across at the Manager, who appeared to be involved in an animated conversation with two young females, about 20 years old, and a male. The three of them left the bar and headed for the exit. On the way out, one of the females drove a big kick straight into the jukebox, and the jukebox immediately stopped playing. Steve was disappointed as he had just put money into it. Two minutes later, the female was back, and on her way in she made a grab for the Telecom phone, which was on a stand.

Steve screamed, "No, no, no, not the fucken Telecom phone!"

This seemed to startle her, and she then turned and glared at us for roughly five seconds, released her grip on the phone, and drove another kick into the jukebox. The jukebox suddenly came to life again and Steve looked at me with amazement and said, "Say what?" We both pissed ourselves laughing and then looked across to the middle of the room. The Manager had the two females in some sort of neck hold and the male was trying to pull the women away, which resulted in the four of them doing a ring-a-ring-a-rosy. It was so comical; but then the aggressive female drove her knee into the Manager's nuts and down he went.

Steve and I decided to step in and help the Manager and as we got there the male said, "It's okay, mate, I'm trying to get them out of here." I knew that's what he had been trying to do. They all left immediately, and we helped the Manager to his feet. On the way out, the troublesome female let rip with another kick into the jukebox, but this time the thing just kept on playing.

I asked the Manager how his nuts were, and he just gave me an agonised distressed look and proceeded to lean face first into the bar with the odd groan emanating from his mouth. I knew how he felt as I'd had a few of these during my football career. Steve and I had another beer and then we both headed off home. I lived about 400 metres from the tavern, so driving wasn't an issue. Just another Friday night at the Cove Tavern.

The months slipped by quickly and the work never got any easier. I got home one day after work and had a beer while leaning against a wall and looking across at the ocean, and I took in how beautiful and blue the water was. I heard the smashing sound of a stubbie coming from the park over the road from our house, and went to the steps to take a closer look. There were two males around 18 years of age at the BBQs in the park, and one smashed a second stubbie into the BBQ and then his mate proceeded to piss on the BBQ. Our neighbours often used these BBQs, as did many other people, and I was incensed.

I took off flat chat to the park and the punks ran off, but I ran one of them down and grabbed him by the back of his shirt. I walked him back to the BBQ and warned him not to try and run away as I would catch him and start using my fists. I reminded him of how brave his mate was and that maybe he should start looking for a more loyal one. Underneath I was seething mad. I made him pick up every piece of glass and put it into the bin, which took a while. After he finished that, I made him take his shirt off. He asked me why he should do that, and I told him to start cleaning the BBQ. By the time the punk had finished cleaning, his shirt was covered in grease, piss, and finely broken shards of glass. The shirt was rendered useless.

The two had come over to Hallett Cove from neighbouring Morphett Vale via the train to have some fun. I warned the idiot never to show his face again in our area, otherwise there would be dire consequences. I never saw them again. I warned the neighbours about the BBQs and told them to make sure they scrubbed them well before cooking, particularly because of the glass problem, not to mention the rest of it.

Brett had come up through the junior ranks of South Australian footy and showed great promise. He played in the same competition as Chad and Kane Cornes, who both went on to have successful footy careers. Brett progressed to playing under 17s and 19s with the Sturt Football Club, and eventually made it into their league side, which was coached at that time by Phil Carman. I did a bit of work for Phil over a couple of years, and he was nothing like the fellow that the press portrayed. Instead I found him to be quietly spoken and a thorough gentleman with a very likeable personality.

Brett and I would go down to the Hallett Cove Oval and have a kick and do some skill work. Aaron would also come along and get involved, and it was clear he didn't have a lot of interest in football but enjoyed these sessions nevertheless. Brett had plenty of natural talent and played some good footy for Sturt, which made me immensely proud. I got a call from my old teammate John Rose, who had played footy with me at Swans Districts in WA (the grandson of Bert Facey who wrote A Fortunate Life). Rosie was now General Manager of the club and informed me that Swans were very interested in getting Brett across to WA to play with them. John said he would be in Adelaide the following week and asked if we could meet. We arranged to have a meal at Hallett Cove and discuss the prospect of Brett venturing across the Nullarbor.

We had a meal and after discussions, Brett was keen to give it a go and I supported him. Alicia was more hesitant as she was losing her baby, which was completely understandable.

Brett was on his way to play with Swans for the 1999 season and appeared to be excited by the prospect. Swans found him a job and he found WA to be a good place to live. I spoke to Brett many times on the phone and while he liked the WA lifestyle, he was hating playing football at Swans because he had no respect for the coach, Peter Wilson, the ex-Richmond and West Coast Eagles player. Brett told me that Wilson was only interested in using him as a battering ram and was not much chop as a coach. I guess his coaching record shows that. I knew exactly how Brett was feeling and tried to encourage him. I told him to stick at it as Wilson wouldn't be around long so far as coaching Swans was concerned. He ended up playing one league game and Wilson taught him absolutely nothing. Brett left Swans after just one season. What a waste of talent. He had a successful football career after leaving Swans Districts, and still lives in Perth today.

The last months of 1999 were terrible for me. I was in a marriage that I didn't want to be in and was constantly depressed about the situation. I would churn over all the negative aspects of the relationship from day one and it wasn't doing my mental state any good at all. There were many days where I would be walking through drizzly low cloud up in the Blackwood Hills in the mornings and I would have tears rolling down my cheeks. During this time, I started to pray to the Lord and asked for guidance and help to ease the pain.

Towards the end of October, I made the decision to separate from Alicia. Aaron was 16 and had one more year of school left, and Brett had been in the work force for a few years by this stage. The house was put on the market, and I had made up my mind to head back to Western Australia when the house had been sold. I told Alicia our time together was over and I didn't want her in my life and that, where I was concerned, her days of manipulation were over.

In early December I came home from work one day and the house had been cleaned out except for the odd piece of furniture and the kitchen table which I had made out of recycled pine. The bed was gone and in its place was a mattress lying on the floor in the middle of the main bedroom. Alicia was nowhere to be seen. The hollow, helpless feeling that I felt at that moment was overwhelming and one I will never forget. I virtually handed the cleaning business over to a fellow down the street who was also in the game, and I continued with the meter reading up until late December. I was left with everything to do as far as the house was concerned.

Chris, my meter reading boss, had organised a job for me in WA with Skill Tech, who were subcontracted by the water supply to read their meters. I had to be back in WA by January 17th, 2000, to start. Alicia finally made contact after about a week and as expected, the conversation was difficult and at times very testy. Alicia told me that she was also returning to WA and would be there before me. It took two weeks to get the house to a vacant possession stage. The agent was left with the job of selling the place. I packed my trailer and Subaru Liberty wagon with everything that would be of any use and pulled out of Olivier Terrace, Hallett Cove, for the last time early on Christmas Day, December 25th, 1999. My beautiful dog Shredder was in the back of the Subaru as we began the journey back to WA.

I stopped briefly in front of the house, looked at it then across to the ocean and felt despair, misery, and sorrow at that moment. I guess one could sum up that sort of feeling as heart sickness or miserableness, but whatever you want to call the feeling, it was intense and distressing. Thirty years of marriage had come to this. What a bloody waste. I had a few possessions and a lot of memories, and at least I had my loyal friend Shredder with me, and we were both about to embark on a new life.

7

BACK TO THE WEST AND MORE PAIN

ON THE WAY ACROSS TO WA, I DECIDED TO CALL IN AND SEE my mate Dommy, who was running the Seabreeze Hotel at Tumby Bay with his wife Julie. I spent Christmas Day with them and stayed the night, hoping to get an early start in the morning. We had a beautiful Christmas lunch of turkey, ham and all the trimmings, washed down with some exquisite Clare Valley reds. If there was one bloke who knew his wines it was Dommy, as he had spent a few years in the industry and knew his wines backwards. This was a late Christmas lunch and we finished it off with coffee and a few vintage ports.

At around 6pm I was sitting at the table and suddenly became engulfed and overcome with emotion. It was a crushing sadness that completely overtook me, and I put my hands over my face and sobbed uncontrollably. Dommy and Julie tried to calm me down, but I could not speak. Don, who lived and worked at the Hotel, went and got Shredder and I went upstairs and retired straight to bed, Shredder slept on the floor alongside me. I left early the next morning without seeing anyone. That night I phoned Dommy and thanked him for Christmas Day and apologised for my episode. Dommy told me not to feel bad and said he fully understood. In fact, he didn't know how I had got this far with all of the drama that had taken place.

No matter how hard I tried, the sadness would not leave me. I was feeling so helpless, but knew I needed to pull myself together and get on with it, no matter how depressing everything seemed. I drove all day until it got dark, around thirteen or fourteen hours, and slept in the car at Mundrabilla Roadhouse.

At sun-up it was on the road again, and it turned out to be a hot day. Approximately 100km out from Norseman, disaster struck. One of the tyres on the trailer shredded, but luck was on my side as it happened a hundred metres from a large parking bay, and luckily for me that day, the parking bay had an emergency telephone. I jacked up the trailer and unbolted the spare and went to put it on. Then to my horror, the bolt holes did not fit. It was the wrong rim for the trailer. For all the years I'd had the trailer, I had never used the spare, and now this. I couldn't leave the trailer and travel into Norseman, as by the time I got back there would be nothing left. The dog and I had about two litres of water left, and it was bloody hot.

I walked across and picked up the phone, which was answered by a policeman at the Norseman Station. I explained my predicament to him, and he told me that he would send the tyre bloke out, so I should just sit tight. I sat there for a couple of hours and there was no tyre bloke in sight. I phoned again and this time a different copper answered. So I went through the story with him.

"Crickey, mate, Constable so and so knocked off a couple of hours ago and he didn't mention anything to me, but don't worry. I will sort it out for you."

I thanked him and let him know I was also nearly out of water. Then around 90 minutes later, the tyre guy arrived in his flat tray towtruck. I had given the copper all the details in regard to the tyre I needed and here was the tyre bloke with a bloody towtruck. Anyway, the trailer was put on the truck, and I followed it to the tyre place in Norseman. Two old blokes ran the place and if they were any more nonchalant or casual then they would have been pronounced dead. They were typical Aussie characters that you would find in remote places in our great country: the smoke (a rollie), a wisecrack followed by a rasping laugh, lift off the terry towelling 100-year-old hat, scratch the head and then put the hat back on.

"Righto then, son, let's get this thing fixed for ya."

"Shit, ya got everything but the kitchen sink on this bloody trailer, mate."

Yep, that was about all I had to show for thirty years, I thought. $475 later and I was on my way. One tyre had just cost me $475. I bade the old devils farewell and headed off to Narrogin to stay with Mum and Dad for a few days.

I pulled into Mum and Dad's place in Kipling Street, Narrogin, at around five or six pm and had no sooner done so when an almighty storm hit. The rain was torrential, and the thunder and lightning put on a phenomenal display of sheer power and beauty, I had followed its progress while heading towards Narrogin. It was always going to be a ripper, evidenced by the sheer blackness of it all. Mum and Dad were very happy to see me, with Mum excited to see her little mazulis, which is Latvian for baby or a little kid. Dad, on the other hand, was a far cry from Mum, and always kept his emotions in check. He would shake my hand and say, "How's it going, Robert?" My mother, father and sister never called me Bob; it was always

Robert. To this day, Ingrid never calls me Bob; It's always Robert.

I had a meal and ended up going to bed fairly early, not so much from tiredness but more from emotional distress, the feeling of sadness and hopelessness. Sleep was the only escape from this awful state. I stayed with Mum and Dad for a few days then headed off to Mandurah to live with my brother-in-law and Ingrid at their place at Halls Head. The stay would be only for as long as it took me to find a place to rent in Perth. I started my job reading water meters and would travel from Mandurah to Osborne Park to go to work.

As jobs go, water meter reading was an abysmal occupation; the meters were hard to find, not all, but a lot of them. A fair few were buried completely, and many were in the middle of overgrown gardens and inaccessible. The Water Corporation had handed the meter reading over to Skill Tech and screwed them down financially, then Skill Tech screwed the workers financially and expected miracles from their underpaid readers. Skill Tech wanted their pound of flesh and the Water Corp were only interested in handing over money to the State Government each year, and of course getting good old pats on the back for their golden efforts. The whole thing was so sickening and what the Water Corp bosses really needed was a kick up the arse for not even being able to run their own meter reading section. At the end of the day it's always the workers who suffer when governments subcontract to the likes of Skill Tech, Serco, and the rest of them.

After six or seven weeks I found a place to rent in Dianella. It was a two-bedroom place which backed onto a church and was situated a couple of hundred metres from the Hotel Alexander, now The Dianella Hotel. The place suited me, and although I detested the thought of renting, it was somewhere to live. I tried getting some semblance of normality back into my life. At least I was now back in Western Australia and would be able to mix with my own family again. I kept on with the meter reading but desperately wanted to get another job. I couldn't stand what I was doing and felt that Skill Tech were taking the piss and getting away with it. The only benefit was that I walked all day, and this took my mind off the rest of my problems.

Alicia was living in Beechboro and Tanya, Brett, and Aaron were also living in the same house. Alicia and I had made contact, so I used to go over on the weekends to have a meal with her and the family. Tanya, Brett, and Aaron were fairly standoffish, but Alicia appeared happy to see me. In around February 2000 our property at Hallett Cove had sold and there was a quick settlement. When we had first put the house on the market, Alicia and I drew up an agreement and gave it to the settlement agent. I had agreed to give Alicia 80% of the funds and keep 20% for myself. Aaron still had one year of school to go, and I didn't want Alicia or him to suffer in any way, particularly where money was concerned. As for me, I was on my own and didn't need as much money as Alicia and Aaron. To this day I am happy that I gave Alicia 80% of the funds and have no regrets whatsoever.

Alicia was keen to get back together again and discussed it with me. I told her no way, as I could not see any future in reconciling. There was no good bringing up the past as that would just cause pain, so we both had to move on. The marriage was over and there was no going back. I kept going over for a meal every couple of weeks, but it was clear that the kids were not that excited to see me there. Every time I went over, Alicia would ask me if I had met anyone yet and my answer was always the same: no. I didn't bother going out and wasn't interested in meeting people.

When I was sitting down one Saturday night at the rental, my phone rang. Ingrid was on the line and asked why I was home on my own. She said that I needed to get out or I would never meet anyone. She banged on about it and finally I said that a few beers at the pub might be good. I got dressed up and headed to the Hotel Alexander. It was only a short walk of 200 metres, very convenient. There was an over-forties singles scene happening, so I walked in and had a look. It was quite busy with a band in full swing and a diverse group of people. For me the entertainment was downing a few beers and observing all the different types of characters. Some were dressed beautifully, and others must have had royal show mirrors at home. I remember looking at a few and wondering how the fuck they could go out looking like that. I mean, they looked so bad, surely they could see that. But hell, who cares; at least it was entertaining.

It was nearing 11pm and I decided to leave and head home. I was never one who liked to go out and enjoy the night life and this was no exception. In fact, I had only ever been to a couple of nightclubs and had hated every minute of it. The loud music meant you couldn't talk to anyone, and the over-priced drinks and falseness of it all just completely turned me off, not to mention some of the blockhead morons that this sort of scene attracts.

I turned to leave and took a few paces when a woman in her early forties stepped in front of me and as I moved to step around, she said, "Don't you believe in saying hello, or do you just wipe people off?" So rude.

I looked at her and my brain was clicking over at a rate of knots as I desperately tried to recognise this woman, but nothing registered. After a pause I asked if she knew Alicia, or whether we had met when I was living in WA some 25 to 30 years ago. The music was loud, and it was difficult to communicate so I asked her if she would like a drink, and we could sit down and talk about what had just transpired, and she agreed. I grabbed a couple of drinks and we sat down where we could hear each other. She told me her name was Shelley and she added that we'd had coffee a couple of weeks previously.

"Shelley, we have never met," I explained. "I have never seen you before, never until tonight. Maybe you are getting me confused with someone else who looks like me."

Shelley was convinced that it was me she had coffee with. It was still reasonably difficult to communicate so I suggested we go to my place for a coffee and have a chat. Shelley replied that it was too risky to go to my place as she didn't know me well enough, and it was something she would not normally do. I finally convinced her that she would have no worries where I was concerned and she agreed.

Shelley drove me the two hundred metres and explained that she lived at Malton Court, which was only about a kilometre away. We talked until roughly 2 am about all sorts of things, including a brief history of each other's lives. She told me that if it wasn't me she had coffee with, then perhaps it was a vivid dream.

It didn't take me long to work out that Shelley was extremely intelligent, she spoke beautifully, and there was something wildly attractive about her. She really intrigued me. That was 15 May 2000, a Saturday, and I told Shelley that I would give her a call on the following Wednesday at approximately 6pm. I could tell she was excited, so she must also have been a little intrigued by me. We arranged to meet at my place on Friday at 6pm. Shelley rocked up with a couple of cans of Emu Export, so we sat out the back and had a few drinks and she also had a few ciggies as she had been a smoker for years. There was a connection between us, and we both knew it pretty much from the start.

I dropped by to see Alicia and the family on the Sunday morning and this time when Alicia asked whether I'd met anyone yet, I replied yes. I could tell immediately that she was not happy, even though she did her best to hide the emotion. Alicia wanted to know her name and what she looked like, how old she was, and where she lived. I told Alicia that Shelley lived in Dianella and worked in real estate in Vic Park. Incredibly, unbeknown to me at the time, Alicia's brother Troy was going out with a woman whose family ran and owned a real estate business just up the road in Vic Park, and this woman knew Shelley. Alicia walked out to the car with me, looked me square in the face and said, "You will never see your kids again." She turned and walked inside and that was the last time I saw her, Tanya and Brett.

Around two weeks later, Shelley received a vile unsigned letter which tore my character apart and made false accusations against me. When I read the letter, I was horrified and knew Alicia was behind it, even though it was not her handwriting. I told Shelley it was all rotten lies. I had a feeling that Tanya may have written the letter for Alicia; even though the handwriting had been disguised somewhat, I thought it was Tanya's.

I got straight on the phone to Alicia and said, "How dare you send filth like this to a person you don't even know and denigrate my character this way! You are just evil."

Alicia, of course, denied the whole thing, but I could tell by her voice that she was lying. I told her I was glad that she was no longer in my life, and I would be attending to the divorce as soon as possible. That was the last time I spoke to Alicia.

Shelley and I started to spend a lot of time together. We were always off somewhere on the weekends, doing or seeing something. We had fallen in love with each other and she started to introduce me to the family. Shelley's mum, Margaret, lived in Nedlands, and was a very proper lady. She was a stickler for good manners and etiquette, as was Shelley, and I loved that as well. Margaret was always beautifully dressed and groomed and one thing that struck me was just how intelligent she and her children were. They all spoke beautiful English and conducted themselves with absolute class. Shelley had two sisters and a brother. Colleen was the oldest and was married to Jack Bannon, a successful engineer and they lived in Cottesloe. Richard was a little younger than Colleen and lived in South Africa; and Jacinda, the youngest, was a nurse and lived in Perth.

Shelley had married at the age of 20 and was thrust into farm life. In her twenties she studied everything to do with computers while working as a secretary-receptionist at a school not far from the farm. Computers were a very new thing in the late seventies and early eighties, and there weren't too many people around that knew much about them. Shelley was an exception and gained a reputation with her knowledge of computers, so much so that New Norica Catholic College asked her to help set up a computer program for the College. She worked at the College and also drove the school bus, ferrying the kids to school in the morning and taking them home in the afternoon. Eventually, she left the school job and helped out on the farm which was managed by her husband. The farm was in the Badgingarra area. Shelley did a lot of work on the farm, including seeding, and cooking for the shearers. She had three children, Ginny, the eldest, followed by Liesel, and the youngest was Kenny. While Shelley had grown up in a privileged environment, she had well and truly shown her toughness and energy during these years.

Shelley taught her husband how to use a computer, and this led him to later acquire a plum job as a purchasing officer in the mining industry. Unfortunately, her husband hooked up with another woman whilst up in the mines, and Shelley divorced him. The husband left Shelley with three children and nothing else. What a selfish individual after everything she had done for him and the crap he had put her through. Shelley moved back to Perth and secured a job with the Institute of Engineers, working in the office. She later went into real estate as a property manager and was working in Victoria Park at the time I met her.

Her son Kenny was living with Shelley at this stage, and he was about eighteen or nineteen. In early 2001, when I was over at Shelley's having dinner with her, Kenny waltzed in and made a smart-arse remark to his mother and then called her a cunt before going upstairs. I looked at Shelley with horror and asked if he spoke to her like that often. She said yes, and that she was having trouble controlling him now. I told Shelley that I just could not sit here and let him mistreat her in this way and asked if she would mind if I went up and had a quiet word to her son. She made me promise that I would not hurt him, to which I replied of course not.

I took my shirt off and Shelley asked me what I was doing. I told her that if he decided to cut loose, I didn't want my shirt ripped, nor did I want blood on it, as it was a new shirt. I assured her again that I wouldn't hurt him but that something had to be done in regard to the way in which he was treating his mother, and the fact that he even did it in front of me showed complete disrespect and a cockiness that I despised.

Kenny was in the shower, so I walked into his room and positioned myself behind the door. He walked into the bedroom, whistling as he did so. He seemed to be very happy with himself indeed. I stepped out from behind the door, which startled him, and he asked what the fuck I was doing in his room and told me to fuck off. I grabbed him by the throat and rammed him into the corner of the wall very forcibly, then took my hand away and told him to have a crack.

"Show me how tough you are, you foul-mouthed creep."

He didn't want to have a go so I told him he was a weak coward, who was okay giving it to his mother but not to a man. I warned him not to ever speak to his mother in such a filthy derogatory manner again, or next time I would belt him for it. Kenny didn't say a word and I walked back downstairs, where Shelley asked if everything was okay.

"Yes," I replied. "All good."

Ten minutes later Kenny walked downstairs past Shelley and me and then turned and called his mother a fucking cunt. I jumped up and chased him. I caught him just outside the gate and threw him violently to the ground, then grabbed him by the scruff of his neck and raised my fist to whack him. Kenny begged me not to hit him, so I pulled him up by the front of his shirt so that he was only a couple of feet from the ground and kept my fist a small distance from his face. He was scared, and I had no intention of hitting him, but he didn't know that. I told him that if he ever wanted to come back to his mother's place, he would have to apologise to her and also to me. And I said this was his last chance with me as next time there would be no talking.

I pulled him upright and then shoved him a couple of metres out towards the road. He walked off to his mate's place and I went back inside. Shelley asked me if I had hit him, and I said no, but maybe I should have given him a bitch slap to wake him up a bit. I asked Shelley how long Kenny had been treating her like this, and she said it had been a couple of years.

After a couple of weeks, Kenny apologised to both Shelley and me for his poor behaviour and we shook hands. He had obviously given the situation a lot of thought and I respected Kenny for his response. After this incident Kenny treated his mother with a lot more respect. Shelley had to bring Ginny, Liesel, and Kenny up on her own, and to this day I admire her courage for the way she battled huge odds in doing so, and for doing such a wonderful job of it. I know how hard it is to bring up a family with two parents involved, let alone for a woman on her own to do it. But Shelley had always had a toughness about her, and she certainly needed it to raise her family alone.

My divorce had gone through, and I'd been with Shelley for about a year. In fact, I'd moved in with her and had been living with her for months. We decided to get married and did so on the 23rd of June 2001. The wedding was held at Jack and Colleen's place in Cottesloe, and we were married by a celebrant. It was a beautiful day, and everything went off without a hitch, just perfect. I was so happy and loved Shelley deeply and was proud to be part of her family. By this time Shelley had taken a job with Ron Farris Real Estate and was doing extremely well, and she convinced me to get into real estate.

A few months before we got married, I put $6,000 into Shelley's mortgage. She didn't have a huge mortgage, so I put what remaining money I had left into it. I threw myself into real estate and was warned that it was a very tough business to be in; but I believed in my ability and was determined to make a go of it, no matter how hard it was going to be. It took about six months to get going on a consistent level, and I really enjoyed the challenges and excitement of it all.

During the early months of this venture, Shelley showed signs that she had another side to her personality, one that I would later refer to as bad Shelley. It would be as if someone flicked a switch and her personality completely changed into a nasty version of Shelley. I just brushed these odd episodes off, not dwelling too much on them, and put it down to one too many white wines.

About five months into our relationship, Shelley and I decided to do a trip to Penang for ten days. This particular trip was the first of many overseas ventures that we would do together. The trip was pretty good, and I remember one night when we were sitting on the balcony outside our room having a few drinks. Our room was six floors up, overlooking the pool. Shelley asked me why I was still wearing my wedding ring and I told her that I couldn't get it off. I couldn't get it over my knuckles and would have to have it cut off. Shelley went on about the ring, which I fully understood, so I got up and fetched some soap and water to try and remove it. I worked on it for about half an hour and to my surprise the ring eventually came off. Not without a battle though. I held the ring up, looked down at the pool to make sure no one was around, then threw the ring into the pool. It landed near the middle of the pool, never to be seen again. There you go, Shelley. I hope you are happy now the ring has gone. Shelley didn't say much about what had just taken place, but she did appear to be satisfied with the whole episode.

The timing of my venture into real estate could not have been better. The Perth property market was about to boom, and Shelley and I were right in the middle of it. It was the early 2000s and house prices were exploding overnight. I discussed with Shelley the opportunity that lay right in front of us. This was a once-in-a-lifetime chance to make real money. Shelley wasn't convinced but eventually came around, realising that now was the time to go for it and set ourselves up for the future.

At this stage I was working with REMAX Real Estate in Midland and doing really well. The agency was run and owned by Max Healy and Jennifer Stageman. These two were larger than life characters with very strong personalities. Jennifer was a gun agent; she was in her late forties, attractive with long black hair, and as determined and tough a woman as you could meet. Max was the big-bellied controller, in his fifties age-wise, with a volcanic personality which he would tone down when the situation required. He could put on the charm and then erupt at the flick of a switch. For most of the three years with these two, I was their only sales rep. The reason for this was that any new rep would only last a short time. I got along like a house on fire with both Jennifer and Max. In fact, it became a bit like a three-ring circus act; but we all worked well together and sold a lot of property. Max's office was a good 10 metres from mine and it wasn't unusual to be on the phone to a client when all of a sudden Max would explode in with such ferocity that I would have to politely tell the client that I would phone back in a few minutes as there appeared to be some form of disturbance outside our office and someone may need help.

At other times, Jennifer and Max would be at each other's throats just outside my office. And you would swear that someone was being murdered. The fracas would soon be over, and Max and Jennifer would be back to normal very quickly, no ill feelings held by either party. I had so many laughs with these two that I really looked forward to going to work each day. They were really good to me, and I guess that I was good for them.

One day, Max walked into the office in a dishevelled state, with scratches on his arms, buttons missing from his shirt, hair over his glasses, and a few dirt marks on his blue shirt. Jennifer and I looked at him and then at each other.

Then Jennifer asked Max, "What the bloody hell have you been doing, Max? You look like a piece of shit." And then we both burst out laughing.

Max blurted out, "It's not fucking funny. I've just gone over in the bloody rose garden."

Apparently, Max had gone to check one of their nearby rental properties and had got into an altercation with a tow truck driver from across the road.

"No Max, I can't imagine you getting yourself caught up in an altercation," Jennifer interrupted.

Max locked his blue eyes onto Jennifer, and you could see he was thinking, "Do I ream her a new arsehole or get on with my story?" He chose the latter.

The tow truck bloke had given Max a mouthful and Maxy had of course responded. The bloke crossed the road and pushed Max into the rose garden and then walked back across the road.

"Jen, my guts got in the road, I lost my balance and took ages to get back up again. I've got to lose some weight; this is bloody embarrassing."

Jennifer and I looked at each other and began to laugh hysterically. Because we were laughing so much, Maxy joined in and had a good laugh too.

After a couple of minutes, we regained our composure and Max looked at me and said, "Mate, I need you to come with me next time I have to go to that rental."

"No worries, Max, consider it done."

I ended up going to the rental on a few occasions with Max, and we never had any drama.

Before marrying Shelley, I had taken her down to Narrogin to meet my parents and I could tell that she was nervous, as one would expect. My parents owned a very small two-bedroom house in Kipling, Street, Narrogin; it was nothing flash but it was their home. I introduced Shelley to Mum, Dad, and my dog Shredder. We stayed that Saturday night and returned to Perth on Sunday. Shelley told me that she found it very hard to understand Mum because of her accent and asked how I could understand everything she said. Well, I had grown up with it so there wasn't a problem; anyhow, the accent wasn't that bad. Everything about this situation was completely foreign to Shelley. This trip had been reasonably uneventful where Shelley was concerned, but that was not going to be the case with subsequent trips to Narrogin.

Jennifer came into my office one day and said, "Mr Beecroft, there is a listing in Ewert Street, Midland, that I reckon you should buy."

That night I discussed it with Shelley, and we decided to buy the property. This was to be the first investment property that we purchased.

Bad Shelley was starting to emerge now and again, and I found it to be really upsetting. The smallest thing would set her off, always after a few drinks, and the personal attacks would start. She would say that she earned more than me and that I was useless, just a fucking useless meter reader, even though I was now in real estate. In my first year with REMAX I'd earned $75,000, but Shelley would try to play down my football career and making disparaging comments such as, "Nobody knows you. If you were any good you would be commentating or on TV. I never heard of you anyway, and nor has anyone else I speak to."

Another favourite was my family. Shelley would say, "Your mother has been in the country for over 40 years and can't even speak English. Your parents were only farm workers, so why do you bloody Beecrofts think you are so good?"

I would get pissed off with these attacks on myself and my family, and would give Shelley a verbal spray then get up and go to bed. Shelley would stay up drinking white wine, but I found it hard to sleep at times when she was really carrying on. On odd occasions I would doze off and the door would open, the light would be flicked on, and Shelley would give me a verbal spray, then slam the door, leaving the light on. She would do this several times. On one of these occasions, I got out of bed and pushed the door shut. The problem was the door jammed the end of her finger, right on the tip. She screamed blue murder and called me a monster amongst other things.

It was a Saturday night at around 2am, and the next thing I heard was her car starting up. I thought, "My god, this woman is as pissed as a maggot and here she is driving her bloody car somewhere." I got a call on Sunday morning, and it was Shelley calling from Charles Gardner Hospital. I drove down there and went in to see her. She had her hand bandaged up and looked strung out. I waited until she was discharged then we walked to her car. Shelley told me that the hospital wanted her to charge me with domestic violence and I told her I'd had a gutful of her episodes and if she didn't pull her head in, I would not be around. Her car was parked at a huge angle across two parking bays, and she got in and drove home. The situation was frosty for a couple of days until good Shelley arrived back on the scene.

I learned to hide my car keys and glasses when bad Shelley erupted as she would hide them if she got them first, and it would take a fair bit of time to find where they were. These odd states of behaviour really worried me, but things would return to normal, and the good Shelley and I would be as happy as Larry.

Shelley and I were making seriously good money and had gotten right into real estate investing; financially everything was going well. Except for the odd episode, our marriage was going strong. We moved into an investment property of ours which was located in Kenwick and lived there for twelve months. In the meantime, we started building a beautiful, rammed earth four-bedroom, two-bathroom home in Madeley. We did it by the owner builder method, thus saving over $100,000. The whole process went extremely smoothly and during this time I also did up the Kenwick property. After a year, we sold Kenwick and moved into our brand-new home at Dainfern Loop in Madeley. The house was only two kilometres from the Kingsway shopping centre and ten minutes from Hillary's on the Ocean—a very good location. The suburb of Madeley is situated 18km north of Perth CBD.

Not long after we moved into Madeley, I was offered a job by Ron Farris, Shelley's boss. Ron Farris Real Estate was a prominent Perth Commercial Real Estate company which Ron had established in 1987. His office was situated at 23

Richardson Street, South Perth, and Ron dealt with a lot of high-profile people in Perth and all over Australia. Ron auctioned off the Telethon home for years and was very well known in the real estate business. Although he would never show it, Ron was one of the wealthiest businessmen in Perth and owned a lot of commercial real estate all over the city. He also owned a huge amount of land at Preston Beach, which he purchased cheaply when the place was nothing. Preston Beach was later to make Ron Farris a very, very wealthy man.

I arranged to meet with Ron in his office at around 6pm one day. I walked in and Ron greeted me with a big warm smile and said, "Hello, Mr Beecroft, can you catch?" He threw a fat file at me, which I caught. "Now, if you come and work for me, that file will be your first listing." Ron told me it was a $1.5 million property situated on West Coast Highway, Scarborough, and the owner had given his agent the flick and wanted Ron to get the job done. Although Ron was primarily a commercial agent, his clients would ask him to sell their residential properties.

Ron needed a good resi-agent and that was to be my job. He would also teach me about the commercial side of real estate. I looked at Ron and saw a bit of Colonel Tom Parker in him. Colonel Parker was Elvis Presley's flamboyant manager. I liked Ron straight away and had no hesitation in saying yes.

"Right, when can you start?" He beamed at me.

I replied, "In two weeks. I need to organise my listings and clean up loose ends first."

"Well, you don't need to look for bloody listings with me, mate. You just need to sell what I throw at you; no time to look for bloody listings."

This was crazy. The hardest thing in real estate was getting listings, and here I was not having to bother with chasing listings. I was over the moon and raring to go.

It was at this time that little Millie came into our lives. Shelley and her daughter Ginny had both gone to the Kingsway Shopping Centre and I received a phone call from Shelley. She had seen a beautiful little pup in the pet shop and wanted to buy the little dog there and then. Shelley already had a shihtzu dog called Mitch, and he was about 12 years old; so I didn't think bringing in such a young puppy would be helpful.

Some 10 minutes later, Shelley and Ginny turned up at the house with this beautiful, tiny white female terrier cross. She had a black nose, black bottom lip and dark eyes, and other than that she was all white. She was so tiny that she sat on the palm of my hand. I fell in love with her immediately. Shelley and Ginny knew I would say yes and that's exactly what happened. They went back to the shop but before they left, I told them I would have a name for the puppy by the time they returned. After a few minutes the name Millie sprang to mind.

When Shelley and Ginny arrived back home with the puppy, I said, "Hello, Millie. Welcome to your new home. Both Shelley and Ginny loved the name and commented on just how much it suited, so that was it.

I was to treasure this wondrous little creature for the next fifteen years. Millie got me through some tough times. Shelley and I had a wonderful life happening and the good times with her were fantastic. It was just so solid and nice. But then bad Shelley would rear her head, and in an instant it would be bedlam and very hurtful. I had no idea why this was happening but when it happened it was just so upsetting.

One episode took place while we were still living in Dianella. My sister Ingrid and brother-in-law Barry had come to visit on a Saturday and were to stay the night. Barry was a good bloke; he had a wiry build, was around five-foot-ten, and had been brought up on the land. He had sold the farm, having had to sell it because of a marriage break-up, and now ran a successful lawn mowing business. Bazza had a nice nature and was a perfect gentleman, and in a lot of ways he reminded me of my father. At around five-thirty we had a few drinks and then sat down and had dinner. Shelley was a terrific cook. She made a beautiful roast, and to this day no one has even come close to the roasts that Shelley was able to produce, they were just so superb. We washed the meal down with some nice wine and everyone was very satisfied with what they had consumed. It was a good night. There was lots of laughter, and we were all having a good time. Ingrid offered to give Shelley a hand with the washing up, but Shelley said no, it was all under control. Ingrid, Barry, and I continued chatting and Shelley got stuck into the dishes.

All of a sudden, in a stern voice, Shelley said, "You bloody Beecrofts think you are so good. God knows why as your parents live in a shit house and were only lowly bloody farm workers. Who do you think you are?"

I was stunned and Ingrid had an angry look on her face as she got straight up from the table and headed into the kitchen. I knew exactly what was about to happen, so I followed her in. Ingrid yelled at Shelley.

"How dare you speak about my parents and family in that manner, you fucking bitch!" she exploded, and with that she went whack, a right sweeping shot into Shelley's ear. Ingrid went to load up with another few but I grabbed her and pulled her away.

Bazza went upstairs and grabbed their case and said, "Mate, we can't stay here after this. We will get a motel." And with that they drove away.

I walked back inside and told Shelley she was disgusting and that she had ruined a good night and it was about time she had a long hard look at herself and to stop denigrating my family. I didn't speak to her for two days after the incident. After this episode Shelley hated Ingrid with a vengeance; another wedge was driven into my family by an out-of-control woman. In subsequent bad Shelley episodes, she would say things like, "Everyone knows you are rooting your sister, and that you are in love with your sister. How disgusting."

I settled in very well at Ron Farris Real Estate and sank my teeth into getting the property on West Coast Highway sold. It had been on the market for about eight months and with a few different agents. Everything I learned of value in residential real estate came from Max and Jennifer and I will be eternally grateful to those two larger-than-life characters. Although at times totally dysfunctional, they knew real estate inside out and backwards. I would open the West Coast Highway property for two hours on Saturday and Sunday, every weekend. The owners were very happy with the job I was doing and commented on the effort being put into it. After approximately three months, I was able to sell the property and both Ron and the owners were ecstatic. The commission was the biggest I had ever received in real estate up to that time. The listings rolled in and I kept on selling them. This was real estate heaven.

Shelley and I would go on an overseas trip each year and we had some great times. We went on cruises, and we went to Thailand, Vietnam, Bali, Vanuatu and Kota Kinabalu, just to mention a few. One thing I did notice with Shelley was that when she had something to look forward to, or a project to sink her teeth into—anything that was exciting—then bad Shelley would not get a look in. She would be the Shelley that I fell in love with and the Shelley that I married.

Not long after we got married, Shelley made a remark that totally astounded me. We were sitting down having a quiet drink and chat when she looked straight at me and said, "You know, you will never get any peace until I die." She gave no explanation for the remark, even though I told her it was a ridiculous thing to say. Shelley denies ever making the remark and she has also denied the fact that I put $6,000 into her Dianella mortgage.

We were waiting to board for the trip home after an overseas holiday and Shelley was going through her usual routine. She had a fear of taking off and landing, so when we were flying she would load up with a few white wines and a small amount of valium prior to take-off. On this particular occasion, she got a bit nasty, and I knew it was only going to get worse as she would keep drinking on the plane. Sure enough, that's exactly what happened. She enjoyed getting me infuriated and exasperated, knowing full well that I would not say anything on the plane. When we landed in Perth I was really annoyed with her behaviour, and by the time we got to baggage collection I was seething inside. We went through customs, and I joined the long queue waiting to grab a taxi. In the meantime Shelley had gone off for a smoke.

I told her that once the taxi was there, I would not wait for her. "Fuck your shit behaviour and fuck your stupid cigarette smoking. I have had enough."

After a while the taxi was available and there was no sign of Shelley. I informed the driver that I was the only passenger and off we went to Madeley. Shelley could smoke the whole packet of cigarettes and get her own taxi—enough was enough.

After arriving home, I grabbed a beer and sat out under the patio desperately trying to calm down. I was looking around the garden; it was around midnight, and everything was so quiet. Then to my bewilderment and shock, I noticed that my stunning feature tree had been brutally chomped by a third, making it look hideous. The tree grew in the corner where four fences met, and it was only a small variety growing to a height of three metres. It cascaded over each fence by a metre and looked stunning. The next-door neighbour Ryan had decided to decimate the tree while I was away. Ryan was in his twenties and married to a snooty little woman that thought she was better than anybody else.

The tree was enough to tip me right over the edge. It was probably more to do with the rage I had inside from dealing with Shelley, but the two issues combined to set me into a real wobbler, a snit fit of mayhem. I grabbed my hand shears and tore into Ryan's frangipani trees which were on a shared border garden. As frangipanis were flying from arsehole to breakfast time, I screamed at him to come outside. All the house lights in the street came on, one by one, but it was clear Ryan was not going to come out.

In the middle of it all Shelley pulled up in a taxi and yelled at me to stop. "What the hell are you doing? Stop it! You have woken up the whole street. Now come inside at once! My God!"

I went back to the patio and had another couple of beers. Shelley didn't bang on too much about being left at the airport as she realised now was not the right time to get into that. I had calmed down and Shelley wasn't displaying any of the obnoxious behaviour that had taken place on our flight home. We called it a night and went to bed. Ryan waited about a week before approaching me in regard to the mayhem that had taken place concerning my tree and his prized frangipanis. He found it hard to believe I'd done an Edward Scissorhands on his frangipanis and painstakingly pointed out how long they actually took to grow.

"Well, it was an eye for an eye, mate. You chomp mine, I chomp yours. You could have discussed the tree with me first, not wait until I went away. Anyhow, I bet my balls your wife got you to cut the tree." Ryan didn't answer that one and all I got from his missus was a few choice words and the finger. Ryan and I shook hands and I said to him, "At least you have plenty of frangipani cuttings to sell, mate—make a bloody fortune." We had a laugh, and it was back on with life.

I was sitting in the waiting area of a tyre shop in Madeley on the seventh of October 2005 when I received a phone call from Narrogin Hospital. Dad had been there for about a week. The nurse told me to get to Narrogin as quickly as possible as she believed Dad only had hours to live. Shelley rushed home from work, and we took off to Narrogin. I was numb and couldn't believe my father was dying. It just didn't seem right.

We went to the ward and into Jimmy's room, and I was gutted as we were too late. Dad had passed about an hour before we were able to make it. Ingrid and Mum were there, and Jimmy looked so peaceful, just lying there in the bed. We sat with him for a couple of hours and then it was time for him to be taken away.

James Alfred Morton Beecroft, born on 16/3/1911, had passed away peacefully on 7/10/2005, aged 94. I did the eulogy at Dad's funeral and afterwards we all headed to the cemetery and then on to the Hordern Hotel. I was so disgusted that not one of my children attended their grandad's funeral. He was such a great man and one of nature's true gentleman. Right there and then I hated Alicia for manipulating and brainwashing my children, and will never forgive that bitch for the rest of my days. Even though my children are now adults, I know that brainwashing stays with them for life, unless they get treatment. On November 18th, 1978, cult leader Jim Jones convinced 900 people to commit suicide, many of them well-educated adults; that is the power of brainwashing at its worse.

In 2007 Shelley got a phone call and she beckoned me to come over. She held the phone up and said, "Bob, it's your son Aaron."

I was shocked as I hadn't seen or heard boo from Aaron for years, and immediately though of what Alicia had said back then: You will never see your kids again.

I grabbed the phone and the voice on the other end said, "Hi Dad, I don't know how to say this but it's your son Aaron."

He was staying with a mate in Bassendean, so I went and picked him up and brought him back to Madeley for a meal and chat. Aaron told me that he had been talking to a few people and found out some home truths about Alicia which had prompted him to make contact with me. He had been living and working in Adelaide as Alicia had moved back there not long after I met Shelley, and Aaron had moved to South Australia as well. Aaron had grown into a good-looking young man, standing around 193cm with an athletic, strong build. He was polite and well mannered, and I was very proud of the young man he had become.

Aaron had met a young lady in Adelaide; it was a serious relationship and they had purchased a house and were living together. From what I could gather, Alicia was putting her nose in where it wasn't required and there appeared to be some friction between the young lady and Alicia. Sadly, that relationship broke up and Aaron of course was quite upset about the whole affair. I kept in touch with Aaron and not too long after this he moved back to Western Australia.

I found out from Aaron that his brother Brett was living in Beechboro and Aaron was in regular contact with him. Aaron had asked Brett to contact me as I was his father, and it was the right thing to do. Brett refused and told Aaron that while their mum was alive his loyalties lay with her; that was his atrocious and dreadful answer. Aaron was very guarded when it came to any questions in relation to Alicia, Brett, or Tanya.

I found out from other people that Brett had married and also had a daughter, my granddaughter. Here he was, my son, not giving a damn about his own father. He just could not care less, didn't give a rat's rectum about me or his grandparents. I wondered how he justified this to his wife. Surely, she would want her daughter to meet her grandfather. It's now been over twenty years since I last saw Brett, and his rotten, selfish attitude just beggars belief. It's up to him should he ever wish to man up and talk to his father again; he is my son, and my door is always open, no matter what has happened in the past or how many years have flowed by.

By 2008 Shelley was managing a huge portfolio of commercial properties for Ron Farris, way more than the other property managers Ron had working for him. Shelley was so good at her job that she kept getting loaded up with more and more properties. I felt this was taking a bit of a toll on her mentally, but she assured me that she was able to handle the workload. It was also around this time that she started to develop orthostatic tremors.

This is a rare movement disorder, and the symptom associated with the disorder is a rapid tremor in the legs that occurs when standing. Walking and sitting are okay as the tremor calms down, but standing in the one spot causes unsteadiness and problems with balancing. Eventually the condition makes it impossible to stand for more than a couple of seconds in the same spot without some form of support.

One day Shelley came to me and said, "Look, I know you have a lot of knowledge with diet and exercise, and I need your help to lose weight." She had ballooned out to 86kg, which was 19kg above her ideal weight of 67kg.

We had a talk and I offered to help her reach her goal weight of 67kg. We purchased a rowing machine and set out a routine. It was porridge for breakfast, normal lunch and dinner, cut out the office crap food on offer, and also cut down on the coffee, and drink more water. Then get on the rowing machine for ten minutes, five days per week, and try to swim or walk on two days of the week. Shelley stuck at it and got to look forward to the exercise. The weight peeled off slowly and after twelve months she was down to her goal weight of 67kg and looking very good.

Shelley was ecstatic and proud of her achievement. I was happy that she was happy, and she was able to keep the weight off for a long time, many years in fact, mostly by just walking and eating well. We started to talk about a lifestyle change as city life was so hectic and the neighbours were too close and all around us. We did a run up the west coast and I asked Shelley why the trees were bent over almost growing parallel to the ground, and she told me they just grew that way up here. Then laughed and said, "No, it's bloody windy up here." We went up to Dongara a couple of times and on one occasion almost got blown off the face of the earth, so that was the end of any ideas about moving anywhere along the mid-west coast.

The real estate market had flattened right out, so after four years with Ron I decided to get out of real estate and told him I had made the decision to quit. Ron asked me to stay and told me that the market would turn as it always does, and just to hang in there. I told Ron that I didn't want to run up a big commission advance bill while the market was slow and thanked him for the great opportunity he had given to me, and I told him how much I had enjoyed my time with him. We shook hands and Ron told me I would always be welcome back.

I took on a job with Gary Tarbet, who owned and ran Lazy Boy Furniture in Osborne Park, and he also had another store near Myaree. Gary was a mad Dockers fan and would talk football at every opportunity. He was easygoing and good to work for. I spent my time on the floor selling, assembling furniture, organising the warehouse and doing deliveries; and then each Wednesday I would head off to the other store and do the grunt work of assembling furniture, setting up displays and moving stuff in and out of the warehouse. The second store was run by a lovely lady called Jan and her younger offsider Michelle, and I enjoyed my time helping the girls out every Wednesday, as they both had a good sense of humour. The job was physical and very busy, and I fully enjoyed my time working for Gary in the furniture game.

Shelley and I had decided to move to Northam for a life-style change, and in fact had purchased a 100-year-old property on one acre of land on a hill only 1500 metres from and overlooking the town of Northam. It was a manager's cottage with a magnificent three-metre-wide verandah running the length of the front of the house and also extending around the side. We had owned it for a couple of years and had a tenant in the property.

The place was run down but I could see it being a magnificent, majestic property, although it would require a lot of work and money to bring it up to scratch. The house was 60 or 70 metres back from the road at 54 Goomalling Road. We decided to take a run up to Northam and buy a property with potential to make money, live in it for a year or so, then sell it and move into 54 Goomalling Road. We found the ideal property at Smith Grove, a small street only a kilometre from town and situated on high ground with views. The block was 2200 square metres, with a cottage-style home on the left-hand side, and in the middle of the land was a big shed. The back of the property had rear lane access. This place oozed potential.

Northam is situated in the wheatbelt of Western Australia, approximately 90 kilometres northeast of Perth in the Avon Valley, and has a population of 6500-7000 people. The town is a regional centre and has all the amenities you would expect with a town of this size, even including Bunnings, Aldi, Woolworths, Coles, and so on. Northam is where the now famous Avon Descent takes place each year towards the end of August, and the town also has quite a rich history dating back to 1833.

I couldn't believe that no one had snapped up this property and the asking price was only $216,000. Shelley and I had a good look inside and outside and purchased Smith Grove there and then. We rented the place out for a while, then I resigned from my job at Lazy Boy Furniture and started work on it. I would travel up on the Monday and stay at the property for four days, then return to Madeley on Friday. There was a lot of work to be done so I got stuck into the place and after a couple of months the inside was good enough for Shelley to move into; but there were still months of work required.

We sold Madeley and moved into Smith Grove. Shelley liked living in the house and little Millie appeared to be happy with the adventure. Shelley was glad to get out of the pressure cooker of managing so many commercial properties and quickly found a job with the Avon Valley Advocate as head of advertising plus other duties. Her boss was John Proud, a very experienced newspaper man who had previously owned and run the Narrogin Observer. John was a portly, easygoing fellow in his very early seventies, with exceptional English skills and a nose that would sniff out a story from a mile away. He was a real newspaper man who would have been at home playing the role in a movie.

Shelley and John worked very well together and Shelley always exceeded her budget, which pleased John no end. She genuinely loved this job, and I was so busy with the house that the months literally flew by. The move seemed to be working wonders for Shelley and I loved being back in the country. This period was very stable and nice.

We decided to start the subdivision with Smith Grove. We would split the block straight up the middle, giving each lot an area of 1100sqm. We took out a few big York gums that lay in the middle of the property and sold off the big shed. The subdivision went reasonably smoothly and took between six and nine months to complete. In the meantime, I started to work on Goomalling Road, and we also got a builder involved as there was a fair bit of building and rebuilding to be done.

I always felt that the Goomalling Road property would be our forever home and the place where we would see out our final days. How wrong that prediction turned out to be. Well into 2010, I decided to get back into the work force and secured a job at Avon Valley mowers and chainsaws, working for Max Hubble. The business also involved swimming pools and everything to do with them, including building new pools. I didn't have anything to do with the pool-building side of the business, but was into the sales side and testing pool water. I had owned a pool in Adelaide for many years, so the pool side of the business came easily to me, but the mower and chainsaw part of the business had to be learned.

Max ran the business with his right-hand man Peter Oliver and Max's wife Stephanie and son Nick, and out the back were two mechanics, one of whom was an apprentice. It was a tight little ship and I enjoyed working there. Max was a robust country bloke who had lived and grown up in Northam. He had a good sense of humour but at times would stray to the moody side and get a little gruff. I didn't care much about that side of Maxy and got on well with him, although there were a couple of occasions where we had a few stern words to say to each other.

Smith Grove was now looking very good and a new Colorbond fence had been put down the middle of the property, separating the block and house. Goomalling Road had its new roof on with magnificent bullnosing running the entire length of the verandah and around the corner. A new kitchen had gone in, and a bedroom had been taken out, making more room for a superb lounge area with north-facing windows right across one wall. This room led out to the back patio. There were four sets of French doors leading out to the front verandah, which was very striking. The property was starting to look spectacular, and I couldn't wait to move into the place.

Smith Grove was put onto the market, and it sold in around ten to twelve weeks for $320,000 cash. We didn't put the block on the market, but that also sold a bit later on for $110,000; so we ended up doubling our money less the subdivision and improvement costs to the property. It had been a very good buy.

Shelley and I moved into Goomalling Road, and I spent every spare minute working on it, a job that ultimately took me four years to complete. I built an entry to the property off Gillett Road, and we named the place Mystique Cottage. The name was taken from a horse that Shelley once owned. I really loved this name, and in fact it genuinely suited the cottage.

Our neighbours across the road were Brethren, which is a Christian denomination that believes solely in the New Testament. I found them to be good people. Whilst they loved a drink, they would never break bread, eat or drink with anyone outside their group. That was no problem for me as my other neighbour Shayno (Shane) drank enough wallop to kill a horse, so I didn't need any more drinking partners.

The Brethren had a little boy called Hunter who was five years old, and three other sons ranging from twelve to sixteen. I was building stone walls down the driveway entry and also constructing a circular rose garden out of stone. It was a lot of work, so I was always out there mixing concrete and laying rocks. Hunter was always over yapping about anything and everything while watching me work. I was always sending him home to get a hat on, then he would dart back. When the circular wall was about 600mm in height, Hunter would want me to lift him over it so that he could stand in the middle, and I would then continue to lay rocks. A few minutes later it would be, "Bob, ya better get me outta here now." So I would lift him out again; and we would do this half a dozen times.

I had an open bag of grey cement and Hunter was perched over it. I had a trowel full of cement and a big rock in the other hand and was in a tight position trying to get this rock into place. I told Hunter on numerous occasions not to touch the cement as it would burn his skin and I didn't want his mum after me. I just about had the rock in place when this little voice says, "Bob, if you don't lift me over the wall, I'm gunna put my arms into the cement."

I looked across at him and sure enough, his arms were ready to dive into the cement. "Hunter, don't touch that cement. I'm coming, mate," I pleaded.

"You had better hurry, Bob."

"Yeah, no worries, I'm just about there, mate."

Too late. The little bugger was up to his armpits in cement.

"Christ all bloody mighty, Hunter! What the hell have you done?"

I grabbed the hose and sprayed him down, all the while telling him how naughty he was. Hunter just smiled and then his mum Amy appeared.

"I hope you are not annoying Mr Beecroft, Hunter," she said.

"No, no, Amy. He is all good. In fact, he is very helpful and good company."

"Well, that's good," she replied. "Come on, Hunter. It's time to pick up your brother; you need to come home."

He looked up at me. "See you later, Bob."

And I'm thinking, Not if I see you first, mate.

Hunter was a funny little fella, and I did enjoy his company—most times, anyhow.

Shelley had to see a neurologist as her orthostatic tremors were getting worse. The neurologist put Shelley on 8mg of Clonazepam and she was also on Lyrica. It appeared to help with the tremors, but the 8mg of clonazepam was too high a dosage and Shelley was to find this out when she changed neurologists later down the track.

Life was very busy during this time, and to wind down a bit we would go on an overseas trip for two weeks. Most of the trips were very good, but on the odd occasion Shelley would blow up and get abusive and threaten to fly home halfway through the vacation, even to the extent of packing her bags and making calls to the airline. She would play this game for a couple of days and would be extremely abusive. These episodes would take the shine off the trip, and would leave me depressed and not wanting to travel with this woman ever again. I hated that feeling with a vengeance.

2011 was a bad year and one I want to try and forget about. Max Hubble was President of the Railways Football Club, and they were really struggling. They had roughly six players who you could call A Grade country footballers, and the rest were very average battlers or B Grade footballers. I decided to give the Club a hand and organised a player's tea where I would address the Club with a plan going forward. This meeting was towards the end of April and very close to the start of the season.

On the afternoon preceding the meeting, Shelley told me that she had been diagnosed with lymphatic breast cancer. I was shocked and felt numb, we discussed the diagnosis for over two hours. I told Shelley that I would phone Max and tell him that I would not be at the meeting.

Shelley said, "No, you have to go. I will be okay. Please go."

I did not want to go to the meeting, but Shelley wanted me to go, so reluctantly I attended it and got home as quickly as possible. Shelley appeared to be okay, and we talked about the cancer again, then went to bed.

Shelley started the chemotherapy treatments, and we would travel down to the Royal Perth Hospital every two weeks, where I would sit with her while the chemo was being fed intravenously into her. It would take around an hour or a little longer. After four to five of these sessions, Shelley suggested that it wasn't necessary for me to be there all the time, so after that I attended now and again. The chemo treatments worked, and Shelley was able to beat the cancer. She lost her hair during the chemo treatment and wore a wig, but in the end her hair grew back beautifully. Shelley is still cancer-free today, 2022.

Shelley had resigned from her job at the newspaper to fight the battle against cancer. During her battle with cancer, all of the lymph nodes had been taken out down Shelley's left arm and she also had her left breast removed. I admired her toughness and determination in taking on and beating this horrible disease. With the lymph nodes gone it meant that the arm would swell to twice the size, and Shelley's shoulder had dropped dramatically. I started to massage her arm every night, trying to get the fluid across to her right side so the body could take it away. As well as this, Shelley wore a tight, specially designed stocking the entire length of the arm, and a special glove for her hand. The next thing we did was to install a pool. It was a 10-metre above-ground pool which was dug in at one end and had decking all around. The decking was the same height as the long front verandah. The pool was situated outside the lounge-sunroom and could be viewed through the windows. It looked really stunning.

Shelley swam every day during the warmer months; she did different strokes and would complete 50 laps and then do other exercises in the water. The improvement to her arm and shoulder was dramatic. It took some effort, but she put the work in and was disciplined. The medicos at Fiona Stanley Hospital couldn't believe how well the arm was looking and wanted to know what she was doing. Shelley told them and they just said to keep doing it, except for one nurse who said to Shelley, "Tell your husband he can't massage your arm like a footballer." I had watched this nurse massage Shelley's arm in the early stages, and she was pathetic, and I told Shelley so. Shelley knew what we were doing was working and didn't take too much notice of this nurse. Later down the track, She was one of the first patients to have a number of lymph nodes transplanted into her arm. These were taken from else-where on her body, and after a couple of months the procedure appeared to work.

Shelley was now back to full health and wanted to get back into the workforce again. She went back to the newspaper job for a few months, but things had changed so much that Shelley started to hate the job. It was getting towards the end of 2011, and I was now doing four days a week with Max; Monday to Thursday with the odd Saturday morning.

I had started to build a gable frame for the large chook pen up the back. It was a Friday afternoon and I'd been at it all day. I was using a 235mm power saw and was up on a ladder. I passed the saw from my left hand across to my right, accidentally engaging the trigger. Unbeknown to me the guard had jammed into an open position, so the blade cut halfway through my right hand. I threw the saw to the ground and briefly looked at my hand. What a mess. I got down off the ladder, took my tracksuit top off, and wrapped the hand up as tightly as I could.

I phoned Shelley and she took me straight up to the hospital; from there I went straight down to Perth, to St John of God Hospital in Subiaco. The surgeon was waiting for me and operated that night. He told me that my hand would never be the same, but they had done the best job they could. I only have half movement and feeling in my little finger. The finger alongside was on a terrible angle, so I had that cut off at the first knuckle; that finger had been badly dislocated twice in one week while I was playing football for Woodville and had given me heaps of trouble ever since, so I was happy to get rid of it.

Early on in the year, Northam experienced a horrendous dust storm. It was towards the end of January. We looked through the lounge windows out in the Goomalling direction and saw a huge red cloud coming in from behind a hilly ridge about two kilometres away.

I looked at Shelley and said, "My God, that's a bloody fire storm and it's huge. Quick, grab Millie and head down the hill and through town. I'll follow you in the ute."

Once outside, we heard trees snapping and cracking like match sticks. The sounds appeared to be around a kilometre away and the sky was red. We jumped into our vehicles and drove a couple of hundred metres, then both realised it was a huge dust storm, so we turned back and drove into the driveway. By this time, we were right in the middle of the storm and struggled to get inside, as the wind appeared to be 150-160km per hour and was extremely difficult to push through.

In the place where my ute was parked prior to leaving, there was now a big gum tree lying on the ground; the tree had been completely torn out of the ground. The snapping and cracking of the trees was very loud as we fought to get inside. Once inside, we secured all the doors and windows and stayed in the bathroom. The noise was deafening. There was a huge bang and a bouncing noise, which we later found out was the cowling from Shayno's chimney, which had snapped off and been hurled along our verandah.

Mystique Cottage weathered the storm superbly and had its new roof put to the ultimate test. The old girl didn't budge an inch. I was amazed at how strong this 100-year-old place was, a testament to the way these old homes were built back then. Northam suffered a lot of damage, as did York; countless homes and buildings had lost their roofs and there were fences destroyed all over town. 2011 had been one bastard of a year, and I was glad to see the end of it.

Shelley left her job at the Avon Valley Advocate and started to put in applications for another job. Life was drifting along reasonably well but every now and then Shelley would have one of her destructive and offensive episodes. We would be sitting under the patio having a drink and talking normally when something would set Shelley off. Sometimes it may have been an innocent remark, but I could always tell by her mood that bad Shelley was lurking just around the corner. Then the shit would start. The abuse was always hurtful and usually involved my family.

I started to record on paper a lot of the crap I copped from Shelley, as I found it hard to believe that this was emanating from the woman I called my wife. A typical tirade would consist of and include utterings such as: "God, it's no wonder your kids don't talk to you." "I feel so sorry for your first wife, Alicia." Or: "Your mother was a thief just like you. The apple doesn't fall far from the tree. She married an older man so she could stay in the country and couldn't even speak English. She was a low life just like you." "Obviously, you were as bad a dad as a husband, so go fuck your sister or her daughter again, incestuous moron. I will not hesitate to make that public." And on the abuse would go.

I would get up and go inside and give her a mouthful on the way in. I would then hide stuff like car keys, glasses or anything I needed next morning for work. After one of these bad Shelley episodes, I went to jump into the ute to go to work next morning and noticed the back tyre was flat. Shelley had let the air out of it and I had to put the spare on. There was nothing wrong with the tyre because I pumped it up at work and it was perfect. Shelley did admit eventually that she had let the tyre down.

These episodes were draining and really depressed me, and at times I would sit under the house for a couple of hours or sit in the shed and wonder what it would be like hanging myself. I would get into some very dark territory and there were a few times I contemplated suicide, but then I would imagine my family and the mess and hurt they would have to endure, and these thoughts stopped me doing anything so awful. The depression from the bad Shelley episodes would go on for days, sometimes weeks. I always hid my true feelings from everybody and dealt with the situation as best I could.

Things would always return to normal, and life was good when bad Shelley stayed away. Shelley landed a job with the ANZ Bank and took to it like a duck to water. She really enjoyed working there. A few months into the job, she met a woman who ran some sort of care facility in Fitzgerald Street, Northam. The facility was funded by the government and had five or six people working there. The woman wanted Shelley to work for her and painted a glowing picture of what the job would entail. Shelley would have to do a six-month course online and then she would be right to go. We discussed the situation and Shelley decided to do the course while still working at the bank. Shelley successfully completed the course and then had to make a decision in regard to taking on this job. She agonised over what to do and eventually decided to leave the bank.

A couple of weeks into her new job, reality struck. The woman had fed Shelley a load of bullshit in regard to the job. The facility was in danger of losing its funding and they had to fill their staff quota. The job entailed dealing with the dropouts of society, including drug-affected people; and it also included dealing with women and children who had fled abusive relationships. She was also expected to clean some of the filthy places occupied by low life losers, and help prepare meals. I told Shelley she should walk out and write a letter to the Government department responsible for the funding and expose the woman running the facility.

Shelley was very upset that she had been conned, and to add insult to injury she had left a job with the ANZ Bank, a job she loved. The facility was eventually shut down. Shelley tried to get back her job at the bank but to no avail, as the bank had hired someone else. She started to put resumes in for all sorts of jobs. I lost count of the number of job applications Shelley submitted. Being overqualified for a lot of the jobs on offer and age discrimination weighed heavily against her. She was 58 years old. Age discrimination is impossible to prove but it was rife and so obvious. Many interviews she had were with smug 30 to 40-year-old smart arses, and she would come home and tell me about them.

Shelley and I decided to subdivide the Goomalling Road property, and this was to be a real challenge and a slog. Several people had tried and failed but we knew it could be done. Mystique Cottage sat on one acre of land, and we decided to chop off 1270 metres squared, running alongside Goomalling Road.

This project would keep Shelley occupied and help with the frustration of not being able to get a job. We hired a good surveyor from Perth and got stuck into it. We dealt with obstacle after obstacle and overcame them one at a time. One of the main problems was the sewer line which ran alongside the fence between Shayno's place and ours. Eventually we created a no man's land around three metres wide, running all the way down to Goomalling Road; this piece of land remained the property of Mystique Cottage. Shelley did a superb job, and the subdivision was completed in twelve months or so.

We also owner-built an extension onto Mystique Cottage at the Gillett Road end, featuring a laundry, a storeroom and a double bedroom with ensuite. The extension was in keeping with the cottage and looked as though it had been there for years. We also purchased another 100-year-old property at Duke Street, Northam, and put tenants into it.

With all this happening Shelley was kept very busy, which she loved. She was such a smart, capable woman, so why in God's name did she carry on the way she did at times? Looking back, I wonder whether she had a mental illness such as bipolar or something else. Or was it mixing too much white wine with her medication? I don't know.

In 2013 I decided to leave Avon Valley Mowers and Chainsaws and take up a position with Serco, working at Yongah Hill, a Federal immigration facility a few kilometres out of Northam that was run by Serco on behalf of the Federal Government. Serco is a multinational company originating in the United Kingdom and it had its tentacles well and truly hooked into Australia.

The company is involved in many contracts running hospitals, onshore immigration detention centres, Centrelink call centres, Australian Defence Force healthcare, rail and bus services, prisons, prisoner transport, and the list goes on. Serco was involved in an incident of fraud involving the prisoner tagging contracts with the UK Ministry of Justice and in 2013 was fined or paid a settlement of $130 million and stripped of its responsibility for tagging criminals in the UK towards the end of 2013; but it is still allowed to bid for lucrative government contacts. The job at Yongah Hill was a real eye-opener for me. Around a dozen of us went through a conditioning course over a six-week period covering all aspects of dealing with detainees, including self-defence and restraining holds which were totally useless. Some of the officers were so piss weak that they wouldn't last two rounds with a revolving door, but in amongst the group there were a few good solid ones.

The detainees were from a lot of different countries including Pakistan, Vietnam, Sri Lanka, Iran, Afghanistan, and many others. In amongst the detainees were men who had just been released from prison and were awaiting deportation. Most of these were real scum of the earth and our government thought it was a good idea to put them in with asylum-seeking detainees.

Serco hid under the banner of "We empower our people" and a few more bullshit slogans; but all they were interested in was always looking good where border force was concerned, and above all the amount of profit they could make out of utter misery. My job was as a response officer, so when a Code Black came over the radio I would attend the scene immediately, along with several other response officers. We never knew what we were walking into and would always be ready for the worst. These were the times when you needed good officers, that you knew had your back. The job was dangerous, especially where I worked, which was in the compounds.

I operated in Eagle Compound. Most of the detainees were good people with stories that would almost bring me to tears. I got to know a lot of them very well. On the other hand, there was a percentage who were nothing but thieves, liars, blackmailers, drug suppliers, and thugs. I saw a lot of misery at Yongah Hill. A detainee had slashed his throat very badly up in Swan Compound, and as I got there, he was on the concrete in front of a Donga, lying on his back with blood pouring everywhere. I yelled for someone to get a towel and the officer with me put pressure on the wound with the towel. The detainee had a hatred of black people, and one of my colleagues happened to be black and he was standing at the detainee's feet. This detainee was in a bad way and spitting heaps of blood out of his mouth; even so, he was still able to protest about the black officer and tried to get to his feet. I motioned for the officer to move away, which he did, and then I put the detainee in the recovery position and waited for the medical staff to arrive.

I saw the detainee three weeks later. He had this huge neck scar, and you could see where it had all been stitched up. I said, "G'day mate, do you remember me?"

"Oh yes, Officer Bob. I remember you, officer," he answered. "Officer, I want to come into your compound to see my friend. Can you let me to come in Officer, Bob?"

"No worries, mate. As long as I know where you are and who you are seeing, that's fine with me," I answered back.

"Thank you so much, Officer Bob. You good man." And off he went.

A month after this exchange, the detainee was dead. He had smuggled oil into his compound and had piled up on butter and God knows what else, and wrapped himself in sheets and set himself on fire. The detainee was taken to Fiona Stanley Hospital, but he didn't make it and sadly passed away.

There were bashings, thieving, smashing of property, drugs and all sorts of mayhem going on at Yongah Hill. I lost count of the reports I wrote while working at the place, but one thing you could not escape was the sadness of it all. A Code Black went off one day and it was for Hawk Compound, the compound directly across from Eagle. I was in the middle of having a wee and the code, as always, sent adrenaline rushing through my body. I thought, "Great! What a bloody time for a Code Black." I quickly finished the wee and took off over to Hawk Compound.

The officers' station had the window smashed and there was glass and crap strewn all over the place. There were five officers there and one of them explained that a big Sundanese detainee had grabbed the computer, picked it up and smashed it through the window from outside the officer station. The detainee had told the compound officers, Meesa Bumfield and

Hamad Shelley, that he was coming back to burn down the officer station. I took off my jacket and positioned myself at the top of the steps ready to take him on—no problem as I had plenty of support from my fellow officers.

The detainee stopped three metres from where I was standing and locked his eyes onto me. We stared at each other for roughly fifteen seconds and for some reason he turned and walked up onto the nearby verandah situated in front of several Dongas. I breathed a sigh of relief that I did not have to physically take this fellow on, and turned to speak with my fellow officers. To my shock and horror there was no one there. I was on my own. At that moment the ERT (Emergency Response Team) burst into the compound, and I took off to block the detainee from escaping to the end of the verandah. I turned and faced the officer station as I got to the end of the verandah and could not believe what I saw next. Scurrying out of the officer station were our officers, Shelley, Bumfield, Hood, and the DSM (Detainee Services Manager), Elane Jordan-Saleen. They ran to the safety of the breezeway or large access way, and out through the big gates that were then locked. The ERT had the detainee in cuffs, and he was taken down to the brig, or lockup. This incident took place in 2017, at which stage I had been doing the job for over four years.

I fronted the officers and called them disgraceful cowards, amongst more colourful language. I looked at Jordan-Saleen and told her that as a DSM she should have led from the front, not rolled onto her back and pissed on herself. These cowardly officers had locked themselves into the toilet and left me to it. I reminded them of what the detainee had told them—that he was going to burn the officer station down—and here were the cowardly fools locking themselves into the toilet. Their intelligence level matched that of their bravery.

After this incident I was put on report for using abusive and threatening language. I had to front the Centre Manager to discuss the report. The Centre Manager was a good bloke and I got on very well with him. He was an ex-UK army man and spoke to me off the record about the incident and the problems with the blue line. Around 30 officers belonged to a particular line, the others being green, yellow and red. The blue line was run by an absolute maggot of a human being named Darion Mudall, and he had surrounded himself with a nasty little clique of people including Jordon-Saleen, who was not only a coward but also semi-literate and on the lower scale of intelligence. Mudall manipulated this clique and they wreaked havoc on certain officers. Eventually the officers resigned because of the bullying from this nasty little group.

The Centre Manager knew what was going on and was desperate to get first-hand evidence on Mudall so that he could get rid of him. The best he could do now was to break up the blue line. I asked him to move me to another line as I could not bear to look at those cowards, let alone work with them. I also wanted this report struck from my record as I was prepared to take it a lot further. The report was done by Mudall and wasn't worth the paper it was written on. The Manager moved me to another line and the report was struck from my record.

While dealing with detainees was difficult, it was a percentage of bad officers that made the job arduous. There was a culture where certain officers would continually snitch or report on each other and some targeted officers had their lives turned into hell. I know of attempted suicides by a couple of them, because of the bullying and harassment perpetrated by the likes of Mudall, Jordan-Saleem, and Bumfield. We all worked a rotating shift system which included day shift, night shift, and days off, and the shifts were 12 hours long.

During this period, I would travel down to Mount Barker now and again to visit my mother. Mum was getting on in age and had been living with Ingrid and Bazza for a few years. She was now 90 years old and about to go into an old age facility in Mount Barker called Banksia, which Is situated right alongside the hospital. It was sad, and obvious that she was struggling; and I knew she didn't have long to live. Sadly, my mother passed away on 31st of July 2014. The funeral was to be held in Narrogin, where she would be buried alongside her Jimmy.

I contacted Aaron to give him the funeral arrangements and was astonished and nonplussed when he told me that he didn't want to get caught up in any family matters or family shit, and would not be attending his grandmother's funeral.

Annoyed by his attitude, I said, "For Christ's sake, Aaron, this is my mother—your grandmother—that we are talking about. You need to be there to pay your respects. For you not to attend will be unforgivable. You call me and let me know what you are doing."

Aaron chose not to attend Mum's funeral. Once again none of my children were at my parent's funeral. I was more than annoyed, furious and disgusted. I had asked Aaron to contact his brother Brett to let him know but never heard a thing from him. How very weak, and totally disrespectful.

I gave the eulogy for Mum's funeral and fought back tears as I looked at the photos being flashed up on the screen. She was a beautiful looking woman in her prime, and she overcame numerous obstacles in her life and gained so much respect.

Benny Fowler was there and was brought to tears. Benny had a bit of an argument with his wife prior to attending the funeral and was so overcome with emotion that he went outside and phoned his wife to tell her that he loved her, and life was too short to waste on arguments or bad feelings. The funeral really affected him, which I found touching. Jaimie Fowler also attended. Mum was laid to rest with the love of her life, Jimmy.

Moving to a new line was refreshing. There was no nasty clique, just officers doing their job. I could work without the added stress of waiting to be called in to front management about some ridiculous, childish report instigated by a fellow officer. This was due to the fact that the fellow running the line had good leadership skills and was also very smart, which is not a bad combination at any level of sport or business.

The only time I saw the blue line after this was when we changed shifts, either signing on or clocking off. The blue line clique would try to intimidate me by the cold long stare or making life as difficult as possible with the changeover, particularly with the electronic wanding and bags going through the x-ray machine. I treated it as a joke. They couldn't have intimidated a pet white mouse, and God only knows how brave they were. I decided to fight fire with fire and started to intimidate the blue line clique. A few weeks later I was notified that my presence was required to explain a charge of intimidation of the entire blue line.

I had a good laugh about it and told them to stick their report, and I said I wouldn't lower myself or play the stinking Serco game any longer. I walked out of that hellhole in 2017 and never went back. I still kept in touch with a couple of my former colleagues and found out that Mudall finally got kicked out of Yongah Hill, along with a couple of others. Serco is a faceless multinational company and has no place doing business in Australia, particularly with its record, and why the taxpayers of Australia allow the Federal Government to employ Serco to run our infrastructure and not run it themselves is totally incomprehensible and wrong. Rupert Soames, Churchill's grandson, had been employed by Serco to be its mouthpiece as the CEO, to try and clean up the grubby reputation and bring respectability back to the company. All I can say to Rupert is: go undercover and work at Yongah Hill for twelve months and really see what Serco is all about.

I took a few months off work then joined Mitre 10 in Northam, working out in the huge trade shed dealing with tradies, timber, gyprock, cement, steel, and so on. I really enjoyed this work, and the fact that it was only four days per week was even better. I would also fill in for people going on leave, and worked extra days when required, which was quite often.

During my time at Serco in 2016, Shelley's mother Margaret passed away. This was a sad time as I got on very well with Margaret and did a lot of jobs for her when she was living in Nedlands. During her last couple of years Margaret had lost the will to live, and used to say that she didn't want to live any longer. She ended up in an aged facility in Bussleton, where sadly she passed away. I was asked to do a eulogy for Margaret, and I gladly agreed to do it. Margaret had a close male friend called Max for many years. Max was articulate with a good sense of humour, and I remember him telling a joke to Shelley, Margaret, and myself when Margaret was living in Nedlands. I laughed at Max's joke and Margaret looked at me with a deadpan face and said, "Please, Bob, don't laugh at his jokes— it only tends to encourage him." That really cracked me up and made me laugh even more. It wasn't so much Maxy's joke, but Margaret's reaction that really got me going. Margaret did have a sense of humour, but not where Max's jokes were concerned.

Margaret's oldest daughter, Colleen, and her husband, Jack Bannon, had put on a spread and supplied drinks for the wake at their Cottesloe home. Margaret's youngest daughter Jacinda had animosity towards Colleen and told everyone that the wake would be held at the hotel across the road. This was a selfish act but no surprise, as that was her character. I still picture Margaret and think of her on a regular basis, as I found her to be a wonderful woman.

Shelley ended up with an inheritance of $220,000 from Margaret's estate. We had a few discussions in relation to the inheritance and I told her it was her money, not mine, and she could do what she wanted with it. We owed $147,000 on Duke Street, while Goomalling Road (Gillett Road since the subdivision) was debt free, or freehold. Shelley decided to pay out the mortgage on Duke Street and buy a secondhand caravan and an Isuzu Mux to tow it, as she was keen to do some caravanning. We did two trips in the caravan and both of us hated it, but the Mux was a good vehicle. The van sat under the lean-to which I had built specially to house it.

8
GOOD SHELLEY AND BAD SHELLEY

SHELLEY'S BAD BEHAVIOUR STARTED TO ESCALATE TO A NEW level towards the end of 2017 and going into 2018. I was getting so fed up with the abuse that one night I wrote a letter on the computer and printed it out. The letter was to Liesel, Shelley's daughter, and I kept it but never posted it. When I look back now, I wish to God I had posted this letter.

The Letter:

Hi Liesel, I'm not quite sure where to start with all of this. Shelley has started to take up smoking again and is blaming me for this happening. Last Thursday we sat down and discussed her visit to Midland Hospital on the Friday and I asked her if she wanted me to take her as I needed to phone work and let them know straight away. Shelley said not to worry about it and that she was not sure what was going to happen, whether she would have to stay or maybe just get examined and booked in for a later date. I went to work and had a very bad incident take place which I was in the middle of and just after the incident Shelley phoned and said she was having surgery and for me to phone at approximately 7pm. I spoke to her that night and she seemed fine and then spoke with her again on Saturday morning. Shelley said she would be OK to drive home and that she would go to Midland Gate shopping centre on the way home which I did not agree with, but she did anyway. She arrived home at approximately 2pm and immediately let fly with a tirade of abuse saying how I never supported her and what a shit husband I was and that I was never there for her. The abuse continued and I did not engage in conversation for some hours, not wanting to stir her up any further. I spoke with Shelley about 6pm and she started to talk and act normally intimating that she wanted a cigarette and that she had purchased some and was going to have a smoke. I asked her not to smoke in front of me as she had not done so for four months, and she was throwing away all of the good work that she had done to give up smoking. Later that night while I was watching TV she started to smoke and is now back to the old habit thus throwing away any opportunity to have an operation to fix her arm and at the same time breast reconstruction. A condition of this important surgery was that Shelley had to give up smoking but now she has decided to throw all this away. The worst part though is that she has blamed me for the taking up smoking again and continued on with the abuse. The abuse had been going on for years and gets particularly nasty when she has too much to drink which is fairly often. Shelley had denigrated my family many, many times and continually refers to me as a useless water meter reader who couldn't get a job without her and how she had to do my Psych test for me to even get into Serco. While I was doing the test, she was sitting alongside me and trying to do the test when in fact I had to tell her to butt out so I could get on with it as there was a time limit, she disagreed with one of my answers and I did change that, but that was it. Shelley has for years taunted me about the fact she earned most of the money and that I was useless and how I had used her by selling Dianella and ruining her life. Shelley has had many interviews for jobs in Northam but has not been able to secure any and she blames me for this as well now, saying it is my fault for making her move to Northam and ruining her life. We both made the decision to move to Northam and the life here is good. Shelley and I decided to make a move to Busselton and put a plan in place to achieve this, hopefully getting there in the next two years. I would be happy to stay here but because she is so unhappy, I agreed to make the move. The problem is that she changes the plan every few weeks when she gets in her mood, and I have no idea what to do about that. Whenever any little thing goes wrong, I cop a tirade of abuse and she says how shitty Northam is and it is all my fault. I also know that her sister Jacinda has been undermining our relationship and Shelley let it slip out accidentally one night, but I had suspected it for a long time. I don't know what Jacinda's problem is, but I do know she is two faced where I am concerned and I have never had it out with her because she is Shelley's sister and I want to keep the peace. every dog has its day sooner or later. I can't take the stress of this situation anymore as I have a very stressful job and with that and the way Shelley carries on it is going to eventually lead to a breakdown which I will avoid at all costs. I still love Shelley, but this situation has become intolerable, and I cannot see any way out of it but to split up and go our separate ways which is what Shelley has wanted for some time now. The roller coaster wave of emotions emanating from this union needs to end for the sake of both of us. I have no idea if Shelley ever displayed the sort of behaviour I have had to put up with to you children as she was bringing you up, but let me say it is not pleasant to suffer. She had a hard time of it bringing you all up by herself without any support from your father and I do admire her for this. Maybe that is the reason she behaves the way she does, who knows. I am feeling very depressed right now and will end by saying how much I respect you Leisel, and hope that you can help your mum get through the next few years.

Love Bob

THE THING I ALWAYS FOUND WITH SHELLEY WAS THAT A couple of days after an episode I used to feel sorry for her. I would look at her and feel so sad, and at times I would go up and give her a hug. It was weird because I well know a few other blokes would have wanted to throttle her for the horrible abuse she perpetrated. Shelley tried to give up smoking on several occasions, and she would last for two weeks then start to want a cigarette. She would then deliberately start an argument, storm off and go to buy cigarettes, and tell me I had made her start smoking again. Whenever she uttered, "I'm giving up smoking," I knew exactly what I was in for.

Shelley's vitriol was the usual stuff, but now also included telling me I was the thief for stealing her mother's inheritance and that Northam was an evil place and I was holding her prisoner here. She would tell me I was a loser and had done nothing with my life, and she didn't want to see me again. A day later, Shelley would deny saying any of this to me. On many occasions, she even told me I hadn't supported her through her cancer or mastectomy and couldn't have cared less, as I would rather go to a football club meeting than support my own wife. She would also say, "You want me dead so that you can have everything."

On many occasions I had talks with Shelley about her episodes of horrible abuse and told her that she was destroying our marriage inch by inch. She would always turn it back on me and say it was all my fault. When Shelley got into one of her bad Shelley moods, she knew what buttons to press where I was concerned, and she got me so angry at times that if I'd had a gun God knows what would have happened. It was that bad, and it would affect me for days. I just prayed that the bad behaviour would end.

On the 4th of June 2018, we sat out on the patio and had a drink and chat before dinner, which was our usual ritual. I would have a couple of glasses of red wine, then have dinner and watch TV for an hour or so before going to bed. Shelley, on the other hand, would have dinner then go back to the patio and continue to drink and puff away on cigarettes. She would go to bed anywhere from 10pm to midnight; on the odd occasion it would be even later, but it wasn't often that this would happen.

On this particular evening, Shelley was in a depressed mood and showed a complete lack of interest in our conversation. When she got like this there was no point sitting there and trying to make conversation as the situation would just get worse. I went to bed at around 9pm and listened to talkback radio, which I would only listen to if I was in bed alone as Shelley really detested it. This was the evening that all hell broke loose with Shelley, and the knife incident described at the beginning of this book happened at approximately 10pm. The police were called and Shelley was taken to Northam Police Station. I went to the hospital to get my hand stitched up. Detectives took me from the hospital to the police station, where I was asked to give a statement, which I decided to do. The detectives told me that I was a lucky man because had I been asleep, they felt I may not have been here.

I felt drained and shattered, and asked them about Shelley. They told me Shelley had changed her story a couple of times and they were convinced that my statement was the correct version of what had occurred that night. The police were up at the house for a couple of hours doing forensics. I got home at 5am and just hugged my beautiful little dog Millie and went to bed. Shelley had been taken to Melaleuca Women's Prison in Canning Vale, and the thought of her sitting in jail ripped my heart out. The feeling of helplessness, uselessness and loneliness just overwhelmed me.

I didn't want Shelley in jail and approached the detectives to have the charges against her dropped. They told me there was no way that would happen and that I needed to realise how serious the episode was, and once again they informed me that I was lucky to still be walking around. I wrote a heartfelt letter to Shelley and told her that despite what had happened I still loved her. I was not allowed to speak with Shelley or see her, and I wasn't allowed to send her anything. I had to rely on her friend Susan Tower and her sister Jacinda for feedback, and to convey the message that I wanted her home and I still loved her, and that Millie and I both missed her.

I shouldn't have been surprised when no feedback was forthcoming as these two women had been undermining my marriage for a long time with their constant negative phone calls to Shelley regarding our marriage. They were both frustrated, negative hung-up bitches anyway, and I disliked the pair of them the first time I laid eyes on them. Jacinda in particular was into emasculating males, and I always thought of her as being a closet lesbian. Two weeks after I had met Shelley the three of us had dinner and as I later found out from Shelley, Jacinda was there to judge me and pass on her opinion to her sister.

Jacinda told Shelley, "He is okay to look at but he's not the sharpest tool in the shed. Well, it's your choice."

In reality, Jacinda was just a frustrated woman who was fast zooming into the realm of being a spinster, and the last thing she wanted was for Shelley to be happy with a man because Jacinda could not attract a decent man no matter what. Susan, on the other hand, was an ageing flirt with a bit of floozy in her, with the blonde hair and the trowelled-on make up and always done up to the nines. She was usually in a relationship, hollow at its best, or breaking up, on her own, or diving into another liaison. These were the two I relied on to get feedback from Shelley; a total and utter waste of time. I was feeling bleak, gloomy and very sombre, and without my little dog Millie I'm not sure I could have gotten through this period.

Paul, my neighbour from over the road, would come across and talk to me for half an hour and the tears would well up. I just couldn't hide the pain I was going through. The neighbours would also drop off occasional meals for me, and I will always be indebted to them for their love and support during this horrible period of my life.

I decided to do an affidavit to try and get Shelley out of jail as quickly as possible, as I was advised that this might help. I visited a law firm in Fitzgerald Street, Northam, and on entering the office observed a woman and a portly gentleman in conversation. They both stopped talking and looked at me.

"Do you know where I can get a good lawyer around here?" I asked.

"You are looking at one, man," the gentleman replied with a South African accent. He introduced himself as Craig and I liked his manner and sense of humour right away. We started off by discussing the fee. We could agree to a set price, or we would use the time method; and after ten minutes I decided that a set fee of around $1300 would be okay, and looking back I'm glad I did because the process took a lot more time than Craig thought it would.

The police report was scrutinised word by word, and the guts of the affidavit was the fact that I didn't believe Shelley wanted to harm or kill me, but more that she wanted to frighten me for some reason. We also tweaked a couple of other sentences, and it was done.

I looked at Craig and said, "Mate, I can't believe this has happened to me as I was married to a psycho for 30 years, and now I'm dealing with another one."

Craig stopped writing, adjusted his glasses down the nose a little and looked at me over the upper rim for about three seconds. Then in his South African accent, he replied, "Robert, there is a common denominator here."

I said, "Fuck off, Craig, you idiot." And we both burst out laughing. It was the first laugh I'd had since the 4th of June.

The affidavit was taken care of, and Shelley was released on bail on 20th June pending a court hearing on 27th June 2018. She had spent two weeks in jail and would have to live with her daughter Liesel until everything was sorted out.

On the 24th of June I received a visit from Department of Public Prosecution; they were represented by David Whisson, who was very high up in the DPP. It was a cold day and we sat in the lounge with the fire burning. The view out over the verandah looking through the French doors was picturesque and with the high ornate ceiling, polished boards and fire going, David felt very comfortable. He commented on what a beautiful property Mystique Cottage was and said how much he loved the old homes with such character. David sat there for around one and a half hours and explained everything to do with court proceedings, likely scenarios, and what the charge of attempted murder was all about. I thanked David for his time, and he left and drove back to Perth.

Even though Shelley was out on bail, I was still not allowed any contact with her. Now and again I would drive to Perth and meet with Liesel at a shopping centre near her place at Beldon. Liesel's demeanour towards me changed dramatically, and she had completely taken Shelley's side. Even though I had explained everything to her regarding the knife attack and what Shelley's behaviour had been like, it made little difference. I was the monster and that was it.

During this period I got a lot of support from Shelley's eldest sister, Colleen Bannon. She would phone and ask how I was going, and we would chat for five to ten minutes, and I always felt better after Colleen's calls. Colleen's husband Jack, on the other hand, never once picked up the phone to say g'day or offer any support. That wasn't a great surprise to me, but it did confirm who had the balls in that union. Ginny also gave me support during these trying times and would call on the phone and chat for a while. She understood the real story and didn't take sides. Ginny supported both her mother and me. Towards the end of September 2018, Shelley was eventually allowed to move back home to Mystique Cottage.

I was told by certain people that I was crazy to let her live with me again after what had happened. They asked me how I would be able to sleep at night and what was going to stop her from doing it again, and said that next time I wouldn't be so lucky. I ignored all of it and Shelley moved back.

Shelley was trying to mask her anger at times when we would have a conversation, and eventually it came out. She was upset that I had gotten the police involved, and that she had been charged with attempted murder and spent time in jail, even though it was only two weeks. No matter what I said, she could not accept responsibility for her actions and she put the blame on me, telling me that I was a sooky-la-la for getting the police involved. Shelley was getting treatment from a psychiatrist, and also had a top law firm fighting to stop her from being sent to jail. As a bail condition she also had to report to the police once per month.

Shelley told me that she wanted our marriage to work and she didn't want to argue with me. I told her that the marriage would work and all would be fine, if she could stop the abuse, particularly after a few drinks. And we both agreed to try hard not to get angry or abusive towards each other. The phone calls from Jacinda were still coming in and she would always ask Shelley if she was okay. Or she would say, "Are you safe? You should leave him." And the rest of the undermining crap that she had been saying for years.

Susan weighed in with her negative calls as well, and both of these women were having a detrimental effect on our marriage. They were being of no help to Shelley at all. In fact, they were making the situation a lot worse. On top of all this, Liesel was on the phone trying to convince Shelley to come back and live with her in Beldon. Liesel was being as nice as pie to me but behind my back she was no better than Jacinda. I had done so much work on her house and helped her out, and this was the thanks I got. I was getting so sick and tired of these women making me out to be a monster and blaming me for all of Shelley's problems. The abuse started up again with Shelley getting into me about my statement to the police being all lies and saying that I wanted her dead so that I could have everything. And on it went.

On 7th of December at 11pm, I was woken up when Shelley entered our bedroom and flicked on the light. She was covered in blood and asked me to take her up to the hospital. She put her arms out with her palms facing upwards and I saw where she had slashed both wrists so deeply that it looked like something out of a slaughterhouse or a Quentin Tarantino blood lust film. It was awful. I jumped up and called an ambulance, then sat her down and covered her wounds with a towel. The ambulance was there quickly, and Shelley was taken to the Northam Hospital then on to Royal Perth Hospital. After visiting Shelley in hospital, I sat down with Millie at home and wondered when this nightmare would ever end. Shelley came home and could not explain why she had slashed her wrists or what she was even thinking at the time. We talked about the medication she was on in relation to her orthostatic tremors and we both felt that she had been put on too high a dosage by her neurologist.

Shelley told me that the neurologist had told her the medication was fine and that he knew what he was doing. She actually had an argument with this fellow and he told her she was welcome to go to another neurologist if she didn't like this treatment. It would be eight years before Shelley did just that, and now the overprescribing neurologist is about to face a fight which may well stop him ever doing this to someone else. I told Shelley that I felt the alcohol could make things worse, and the mixing of these drugs with alcohol might not be a good thing. We tried to get on with life, but it just wasn't working out at all. On 6th January at approximately 5:30pm, I had just come out of the shower and had a towel wrapped around my waist when I heard Shelley talking on the phone. She has a clear, strong voice, and I heard my name mentioned.

She was talking to her psychiatrist and told him that she was making plans to move out as she had been advised by others. She didn't inform him that "others" meant her sister Jacinda and the worthless Susan urging her to move out of the house as it was unsafe to be with me. Shelley went on to say that she had slashed her wrists and had been admitted to RPH and that her lawyer had told her that Bob wanted her to kill herself so that he could have everything. She said that her lawyer had also advised her to get out.

I got dressed and by this time Shelley was off the phone. I told her that I was sick and tired of her making me out to be a monster and shifting the blame for her destructive behaviour onto me. I told her that I was the one that had to get out of this relationship just to preserve my sanity, and that she had turned our marriage into an arduous and hellish situation. I also reminded her that I was the one who should be feeling unsafe in light of what had taken place. I told her then and there that it was over between the two of us. Shelley got onto the phone and ranted to her daughter Liesel that I was to blame for everything.

The very next night at 7:45pm, Shelley started another tirade of abuse as I was sitting down watching TV. She came in from the patio and started spewing her venom.

"I can't stand looking at a low life thief. You are such a liar. You have stolen my inheritance." She went back out on to the patio and continued drinking.

Ten minutes later I walked out to the patio and told Shelley to contact the local settlement agent. I said I would sign Duke Street over to her. And I added that I wasn't interested in touching one red cent of her mother's inheritance and Duke Street was worth a lot more that the inheritance, and at least now I wouldn't have to listen to the abuse regarding the inheritance. I then walked inside and went to bed. This woman was starting to drain the very life out of me. Shelley wasted no time in getting the paperwork drawn up and I signed Duke Street over to her. She was to do very well out of this transaction.

On 17th January 2019 at 7:30pm, I protested to Shelley about the constant negative calls coming in from her sister Jacinda and her fake friend Susan; and now her daughter Liesel was also on the bandwagon. It was the usual crap. Are you safe? You need to leave him. And on they would go. I told Shelley that she needed to tell these women to butt out and stop their rubbish. Shelley left the next morning and went to stay with Liesel.

On 29th January I got a call from one of the Northam detectives on behalf of the Department of Public Prosecutions. He wanted to know what my feelings were in regard to the upcoming court case concerning Shelley. I informed him that I would not give evidence against Shelley and that it would be ridiculous of me to prosecute her as she had been living at home for months and I did not want her to go to jail. The detective was going to discuss my thoughts with David Whisson, and he felt that the charge of attempted murder would most likely be downgraded or it could be dropped. This conversation took place in the morning.

I phoned Shelley and advised her of the conversation, and she sounded very relieved and thanked me for doing this. I drove down to Bassendean Oval to attend the funeral of one of Swans Districts great past players, Fred Castledine. Freddy was a Swans Hall of Famer and had played in three Premierships in 1961, 1962 and 1963. On my way home at around 5pm I received a call from Shelley, who was still living at Liesel's.

I was just approaching Bakers Hill so pulled in and spoke with her. Initially it was just general chit-chat and then she informed me that she would not come home to help with the sale of the house because I had put restrictions on who could call her. I replied that I was sick and tired of being made out to be a monster by her, and sick to death of the negative calls from her sister Jacinda and the moron Susan, and also her daughter Liesel.

Shelley said that husbands don't charge their wives with attempted murder or even get the police involved. Shelley then told me her friend Rhonda had stabbed her husband in the back with a pair of scissors and that he didn't get the police involved. Rhonda was a psycho friend of Jacinda and Shelley who, along with Jacinda, loved to emasculate males. Unfortunately, I met this idiot of a woman once and there will not be a second time.

I replied to Shelley by saying that maybe her stupid friend should have used a 30cm butcher's knife instead of scissors, and I reckon the police would well and truly been involved then. As usual the conversation deteriorated, with Shelley saying I had covered her with bruises and pushed her to the ground. This was in reference to an incident which took place just before she went off to Liesel's. At no time was Shelley pushed to the ground, but it would have sounded dramatic to her sister, daughter and Susan, or whoever else wanted to listen. The big bad monster had struck again. What happened was that Shelley had located and taken the yellow file in which I had been storing notes on her awful behaviour. She would not give me my file, so I grabbed her laptop and refused to hand it to her until she gave me my file back. Shelley came at me a few times trying to get the laptop, and as this was going on she sustained a couple of bruises to her arm as I grabbed it to fend her off. I managed to snatch my file from her and then handed the laptop back.

I told Shelley that telling people she had been pushed to the ground was a malicious lie and she needed to stop her nonsense. I informed Shelley that I had been going out on a limb for her in order to save her a stint in jail, and if I was a monster then I would have done my best to put her inside, not defend her. Shelley just flew into a tirade of vitriol and told me she couldn't care less if she ended up in jail. She was very adept at playing the victim and getting people to feel sorry for her, including me. She portrayed vulnerability so effectively that you would find yourself feeling sorry for her.

On 13th of February 2019, Shelley went to Busselton for five days to stay with Jacinda for a break, and then returned to Liesel's. She had an appointment with her lawyer on the 20th of February and also an appointment with her psychiatrist. I phoned Shelley at 6:30pm on the 20th of February and she was in a bad mood and appeared to be depressed. Shelley said she could not go to trial as the waiting and not knowing what was going to happen was all too much. She told me that she was too old to go through this crap and would not be around anyway.

I asked her where she would be, and she answered with: "I will not be around. I don't have a life, only a shit one. I never have any fun and I'm too old so I won't be around."

I tried to calm her down and reminded her that the DPP were going to recommend a non-custodial sentence, and everything would work out okay.

I was in another phone conversation with Shelley on 21st of February at about 8pm. We spoke about her coming home and trying to live a normal life and to get through this mess. Shelley told me that she wanted to come home but if she did all hell would break loose, so I asked her why that would be the case. She said her sister would be furious and so would her daughter Liesel. I told Shelley that her frustrated sister had been trying to break the marriage up for years and now Liesel was also at it; and if I never laid eyes on Jacinda again for the rest of my life it would be too soon.

Shelley said she would be home on Saturday regardless of what her sister and daughter thought. She said, "I want to come home." She came home and for over a week she appeared to be happy and normal again, but it wasn't to last.

On the 5th of March 2019 we sat down under the patio before dinner and all of a sudden Shelley told me that I had ruined her life by making a statement to the police, and I had acted like a big girl by going over to the neighbours after the knife episode. She had been in a bad mood all day. I had put the dishwasher on in the morning and according to her it was only half full. She said that I had made her so angry by doing this, and she just would not let it go. We had gone shopping after that, and at the checkout the fellow in front of us was putting his stuff on the checkout conveyor and Shelley grabbed the divider and put it at the back of his shopping. The only problem was he still had some items in his trolley and Shelley hadn't left him any room. I pulled the divider back to give him more room and Shelley flew into me with abuse and then would not speak to me.

When eventually she did speak to me hours later, it was only to fire more abuse, so I just got up and went inside. I went to bed at around 10pm and Shelley followed at 11pm. She went on and on with abusive language, so much so that I had to get up and sleep in another bedroom. A couple of days later Shelley was still in her horrible mood, so I went and sat on the front verandah for a bit of peace. At about 9:30pm she emptied the trophy cabinet of all its contents. Lying on the floor were all my footy memorabilia, trophies, medals, photos, etc. She told me that she did not want my shit in her cabinet. I pointed out that it was our cabinet not solely hers, but there was no reasoning with her. It was her cabinet and that was it. Shelley got on the phone to Jacinda, then Liesel, and told them what a prick I was and that she would be glad when the house was sold.

On the 25th of March 2019, I handed a signed statement to David Whisson at the DPP. The statement read:

I Robert James Beecroft wish to advise the DPP that I do not want this matter to go to trial and that I will not give evidence. I acknowledge that my police statement is true, and my affidavit is also true.

Shelley's trial took place, and she was handed a suspended sentence of eighteen months and had to report to a parole officer once a month for this period of time. She was now free to resume with her life and we decided to give the marriage one more try.

Mystique Cottage sold on 10th May 2019, and we moved into Shelley's house at Duke Street, Northam. I had started to do a lot of work on the property in the preceding few months as our tenants went to Perth and we decided not to put any more tenants in, as Mystique Cottage was on the market and I needed to work on the property. I landscaped the front, put in gates front and back, built fences front and back, repolished the floors and painted etc. The property came up a treat and it was a very comfortable place to live in. I never ever wanted to sell Mystique Cottage, but Shelley was not happy there. God knows why as it was a magnificent property. Shelley was always rattling on about the property being too big and too much to look after. I could never understand this as I did everything outside and always cleaned the house with Shelley. I would clean the two bathrooms and vacuum then wash all the floors. Shelley wanting to sell Mystique Cottage frustrated the hell out of me and one time I told her that I doubted she would be happy anywhere.

We settled into Duke Street, and I continued to work on the property as well as working in my job at Mitre 10. Things rolled on without too much drama for a couple of months, but the serenity did not last. Shelley just could not accept or take responsibility for what she had done, and out of the blue would rip into me saying that I had put her in jail, and I had ruined her life, and how could I do this to her, and on it would go, straight back into the old pattern of behaviour.

One afternoon Shelley received a call from her parole officer, who asked her if she was still living with the victim. This question sent Shelley into a very nasty mood which just got darker as the day progressed. I arrived home from work and it didn't take long for the bad Shelley to rear her head. She let loose with the statement that she was the victim, and then followed up with: "How dare you put me in this position?" And she continued on with an offensive diatribe of language. Shelley then went into the kitchen, grabbed my dinner and walked out to my ute and threw the whole lot over the windscreen.

This incident took place on Monday the 2nd of September. On the Tuesday I went to work and came home at around 5:30pm, and the atmosphere was very sullen indeed. Shelley went and sat on her own in the enclosed courtyard situated near the kitchen, and I sat out on the patio as usual. At approximately 7:30 pm, I went into the kitchen and took my dinner out onto the patio and ate the meal there. Just as I finished eating, my mobile phone went off and I noticed that it was Liesel calling. Liesel started chatting normally and nicely, which I found very odd in light of what had taken place and her subsequent attitude towards me. But nevertheless I kept talking with her.

During the conversation I got up from the table to take my plate inside and went to open the door. It was locked. I knocked on the door and yelled out for Shelley to open it but there was no answer. During this, Liesel was still on the phone so I went back to the patio table and sat down. I informed Liesel that Shelley had locked me out of the house for no reason. Just then I heard my name being called out by a male voice and told Leisel that someone was there, and I had to go.

All of a sudden there were cops everywhere and three of them came up onto the patio. I asked them what the hell was going on and they told me Shelley had phoned them in a distressed state claiming that I was going to break her jaw. I told them that Shelley had locked me out of the house for no reason and that I had yelled out for her to open the door. The officers were very good and said they realised Shelley had mental problems. They said that I could not stay in the house with her on this night and I would have to sleep elsewhere, and asked if I had somewhere else to sleep for the night.

I told them that I didn't so I would sleep in my ute for the night. I grabbed a doona off my bed and ended up trying to sleep in the ute down at the sports ground near McDonalds. The temperature dropped to -1 degree Centigrade, which was common for this time of the year, and I was lucky to get two hours sleep.

I remember walking past Shelley at the front door and she had an expressionless look on her face. I paused and looked into her eyes and said, "This is the last straw, Shelley. You will pay for this."

There was no answer from her, and she remained expressionless. I got back to the house at around 6am and went straight to bed and woke up at midday. Shelley was in the kitchen, and I refused to speak with her.

She looked at me and coldly said, "Get out of my house."

I replied that I certainly would and would be out in a few days.

Ingrid and Barry needed someone to look after their house in Mount Barker as the tenants had left and they were desperate for the home to be occupied and maintained. I explained what had taken place and agreed to live in the house. I loaded the ute to the hilt and drove off to Mt Barker, a trip of four hours. I told Shelley that I would be back in two days to pick up the final load, which I did. On the 10th of September 2019, I moved into the house at Mt Barker. This was to be a very lonely and sad period, especially the first couple of months.

On 21st of September 2019, Shelley phoned and told me Millie had fallen down the steps and had injured her shoulder badly. Millie was around 14 years old and Shelley had to have her put down. I was devastated and had tears rolling down my face. My beautiful little Mill Mill, who had gone through so much with me, was now gone. I found it so hard to come to terms with. Not only was I trying to deal with all the emotion of the situation with Shelley, but now my little dog was gone as well.

I was completely on my own and suffering this unbearable sadness. I needed something to take my mind off the misery so decided to join the Mt Barker Golf Bowling Club, which turned out to be a blessing. Barry and Ingrid were good friends with the President, Syd Anning, so I wandered up to the Club on a Sunday for off-season scroungers and introduced myself to Syd. The members were all very welcoming, and I settled in quickly. Besides bowls, I rode my bike on 23km runs and lifted weights, plus I maintained Ingrid and Barry's house, which was on a large block.

Shelley would phone or text reasonably often and a lot of the time the texts or calls would end up in a clusterfuck, some-thing I definitely didn't need. The bowls pennant season was about to start, and I was selected to play first division. I'd only been playing bowls for a couple of years, so it was a huge deal to be selected in first division. Our first game was at Denmark, a picturesque coastal town around 400km southeast of Perth and 47km from Mt Barker. Fifteen minutes before the game I received a call from Shelley. She sounded distressed and was crying, telling me that she could not cope on her own and there were a few problems that needed fixing at Duke Street, and the garden was getting out of control, and on she went. I told her to settle down and said that I would call her when I got home from Denmark.

The call made me feel horrible and I just felt like dropping to my knees and screaming. When would this nightmare end? I can't remember what happened with bowls that day, but I phoned Shelley as soon as I got home. I agreed to drive to Northam and do the gardens and also attend to the maintenance issues. This would be one of four such trips. After these trips, Duke Street looked a picture, as the main issue was the gardens, and other small jobs were easily taken care of.

Talking to Shelley, I could sense her sadness with the whole situation and the fact she should never have behaved the way she did, but it was all too late for me. Shelley wanted us to get back together again but I told her there was no chance as I could not trust her to behave, and I would never put myself through that type of hell again. I also informed Shelley that I could not keep driving to Northam every time the gardens needed doing and that she would have to pay someone to do them.

Shelley told me that she intended to sell Duke Street and move into an over-55s lifestyle village north of Wanneroo. In February 2020, the house at Duke Street Northam sold for $258,000, a lot more than the inheritance of $220,000.

Did Shelley split the difference with me? Not on your nelly. I made one final trip to Duke Street as Shelley had asked me to pick up pot plants and other items that the removalists could not fit into their truck. I did this for her and took the load to Shelley's new place, stayed the night in her spare bedroom, and returned to Mt Barker the next day.

Barry had secured a job in Mount Barker as curator of the racetrack and was going to move down from Kalgoorlie to take up the position while Ingrid stayed in Kalgoorlie taking care of the sale of their property. When Bazza moved back it was good to have someone to talk to, particularly as Shelley was texting me at least once or twice per week with stuff like: You have broken my heart and my spirit, You are a redneck lying dork, You are a non-person who is useless and robotic with a heart of stone, or Robert it is costing me $80 to have the lawns mowed, you really have ruined me. Shelley had never called me Robert in 20 years. Sometimes the texts would be happy and nice ones which would make me feel good, but then they would get nasty a week later and it was back to down in the dumps.

The racetrack was creating dramas, particularly with the retic blowing up all over the place, and I was spending a lot of time helping Bazza. In fact, the job had become a nightmare even though we were putting everything into it, and after twelve months Bazza resigned from the position, a decision he never regretted.

In October 2019 I spotted a rundown 100-year-old cottage in Muir Street, Mount Barker, and would sit and look at it and mentally renovate the property. I decided to buy the place, and I started the renovation in December of 2019.

There was an enormous amount of work to be done and I threw myself into the job, firstly making a huge list of everything needing to be done and then crossing each job off one at a time. The work kept me occupied and gave me little time to think about the past. I had a mental picture of what the cottage should look like and set about bringing the picture to reality. Every spare minute I had was used to bring the Muir Street house back to its former glory, starting with the inside first. The thing with a house like this is, you cannot let the work overwhelm you. It's important to start one job and finish it completely before going on to the next one, and eventually you start to notice the progress and transformation, which tends to be uplifting and energising.

Once the inside was done it was onto the outside. I land-scaped the front and back, rebuilt the verandah, built canopies over windows, secured the back with a shed and a beautiful big solid white gate, and painted the whole house by brush. The horrible patio at the back was taken down and Bazza and I built a 60-metre squared gabled patio to replace it. The place came up so well that it surprised even me on completion of the renovation. The job had taken approximately eighteen months. The white picket fence and David Austin roses finished the home off beautifully. I named the house Millie's Cottage after my adorable, cute little dog Millie, whom I still miss enormously.

Shelley and I finally divorced on 25th November 2021. Except for bad Shelley, she was the woman that I wanted to live with for the rest of my life. Everything I looked for in a woman Shelley had, and to this day we still love each other but we both know we could never live together again. Shelley and I accomplished many great things together and had a lot of truly enjoyable fun times with each other, but bad Shelley was like a Chucky doll; when it came out there was only mayhem and destruction, all bad stuff, but then Chucky would go away for a while and things would be good.

To this day I still haven't gotten over the sadness of it all. I always remember taking my last load of possessions to Mt Barker. Shelley was very quiet and had a look of sadness about her, almost as if she believed that I would never actually leave. She had told me years before that she would be devastated and totally gutted if I ever left her, and now that the day had finally arrived, I sensed the pain she was feeling. I somehow felt at that moment that she would give anything to take all the bad behaviour away and start again. I also thought that maybe she couldn't control the bad stuff, and maybe it was just a part of her personality. I felt a wave of sadness right there and I'm sure she did too. My pain would begin to manifest itself soon enough. Here I was again carting my possessions, but it was now time to start thinking of myself and start to respect and love myself for a change.

I looked at this as beating the enemy by saying no, having the strength to say no more will I suffer this kind of life, and now was the time for change. I came to the realisation that to stay with Shelley would lead me into more pain, and God knows I had suffered enough. I knew deep down that I could never ever change Shelley and right now I had to love me more than her, as the torment of staying would be far greater than that of walking away. The strength to make the awful decision came from deep within and I would need every ounce of it to deal with the ensuing harrowing emotions that would invade and consume me many times over the next eighteen months.

The early months at Mount Barker were not only lonely but also emotionally draining. I thrashed myself on my bike, walked, lifted weights, looked after Ingrid and Barry's huge garden—anything to get my mind off this awful situation. I would tell myself many times a day that the decision was the right one and the alternative would be horrible. This time I needed to take care of myself. Time would eventually heal the pain of it all. I had done it once and I could do it again, although this time around the woman I had left was one that I truly loved and wanted to spend the rest of my life with. The situation was going to be harder to overcome but I needed to stay strong and true to myself. Now, looking back, I can see that the decision I made was the right one and my life is now what I would term "normal", if there is such a thing. Never again will I allow myself to be dragged through emotional hell. I finally have too much respect for myself. Do I still love Shelley? Yes, I do, but only good Shelley. Separating good and bad Shelley, I realise, would be impossible as bad Shelley would always be around and I don't ever want to be near bad Shelley again.

The cottage has been a saviour. The many good mates I have at the bowling club have made this part of the journey a little easier, and reuniting with my old mates at Swan Districts Football Club has also been good for me. My sister Ingrid and brother-in-law Bazza have both been a big support through trying times. I have gone through the rapids of life and finally hit calmer water at 70 years of age. Whenever I need inspiration or a lift in spirit, I always go back to my football experiences, which encompassed all the emotions and physicality one needs to get through the hard parts of life. Everyone suffers one way or another in life, but it's how you deal with it that truly defines character. I pray to God each day and thank Him for my life. I have nothing to complain about. I look back with pride at a small boy's dream to play football at the highest level. Yes, dreams do come true.

Milton Keynes UK
Ingram Content Group UK Ltd.
UKHW010853040923
428018UK00004B/496